Uncovering Hidden Treasures of Scotland's Past

Maliha .T Hayes

All rights reserved.

Copyright © 2024 Maliha .T Hayes

Uncovering Hidden Treasures of Scotland's Past : Exploring Scotland's Rich History: Discovering Secrets Buried in Time

<u>Funny helpful tips:</u>

Your dreams are the wings that propel you forward; nurture them with dedication and belief.

Your potential is a treasure waiting to be unearthed; dig deep and discover your true capabilities.

Embark on a journey through time, beginning with the turbulent period of "Medieval Strife." Witness the rise of Kenneth MacAlpin, King of the Picts, and delve into the intriguing tale of Macbeth, the regicidal king. Uncover the emergence of the Scottish nation-state and explore its golden age, marked by significant cultural and historical developments.

Dive into the epic struggles of the Wars of Independence, and examine the impact of the Black Death on the course of Scottish history. Traverse the House of Stewart's reign and encounter the enigmatic figure of Mary, Queen of Scots, often referred to as "The Daughter of Debate."

As Scotland's history intertwines with broader British narratives, the guide navigates the complex dynamics of the Union and the Scottish Enlightenment. Transitioning into the Industrial Revolution, witness the transformation of Scotland's landscape and society.

Contents

Part 1: Scottish History 1
  A Captivating Guide to the History of Scotland 1
  Chapter 1 – Medieval Strife 2
  Chapter 2 - Kenneth MacAlpin, King of the Picts 6
  Chapter 3: Macbeth, the Regicidal King 10
  Chapter 4 – The Emergence of the Scottish Nation-State 13
  Chapter 5 – The Golden Age 19
  Chapter 6 – The Wars of Independence 23
  Chapter 7 – The Black Death 29
  Chapter 8 – The House of Stewart 32
  Chapter 9 – Mary, Queen of Scots: "The Daughter of Debate" ... 36
  Chapter 10 – The King of Great Britain 43
  Chapter 11 – The Union and The Scottish Enlightenment 47
  Chapter 12 – The Industrial Revolution 52
  Chapter 13 – Decline 57
  Chapter 14: Scottish Feminism 60
  Chapter 15: LGBT Rights in Scotland 65
  Chapter 16: The Loch Ness Monster 69
  Chapter 17: Postwar Scotland 73

Part 2: Wars of Scottish Independence 78
  Chapter 1 – Good Fences; Good Neighbors 79
  Chapter 2 – Crisis 83
  Chapter 3 – Defiance 88
  Chapter 4 – The Martyr 95

- Chapter 5 – Power Struggles 113
- Chapter 6 – Inner Strife 117
- Chapter 7 – The Battle of Bannockburn 122
- Chapter 8 – A Worthy King 127
- Chapter 9 – Where Your Heart Is 132
- Chapter 10 – The Son of the Bruce & the SecondWar for Independence........134

Part 3: William Wallace 153
- Chapter 1 – Mysterious Origins..154
- Chapter 2 – Coming of Age in Crisis 158
- Chapter 3 – Defiance and Compliance 163
- Chapter 4 – The Prophecy 169
- Chapter 5 – Uprising 173
- Chapter 6 – Love in a Time of War..177
- Chapter 7 – The Battle of Stirling Bridge..180
- Chapter 8 – Invading England...186
- Chapter 9 – The Guardian of Scotland..189
- Chapter 10 – Defeat at Falkirk 193
- Chapter 11 – An Outlaw Once More..196
- Chapter 12 – The Execution...201

Part 1: Scottish History
A Captivating Guide to the History of Scotland

Chapter 1 – Medieval Strife

To envision what Scotland's earliest history looked like, you must make the effort to consciously imagine a time long before there was a heavily urbanized population. There were no road networks in existence, nor a string of towns and cities connected by frequent trade. The forests were all uncleared, the bogs were filled to the brim, and the heavily mountainous terrain prevented easy migrations up, down, and across the lands. The Highlands (to the north and west), which contained most of Scotland's hills and mountains, were far less hospitable than the flatter and more fertile Lowlands (to the south and east).[4]

Most long-distance travel and trade would have been achieved by water, along Scotland's ten major rivers, numerous firths, and its extensive coastline. The majority of Scotland's earliest inhabitants toiled in one form of agriculture or another, helping to ensure that their local area could produce all the food and goods it needed to be self-sufficient. One's wealth and happiness largely depended on the fertility of the land that one had access to, as well as one's industriousness in extracting subsistence from it.

The Scottish terrain only became inhabitable to people towards the end of the last glacial period (c. 115,000 – c. 11,700 years ago).[5] Much of North America was blanketed by ice during this time, while the Scandinavian ice sheet extended its reach into the northern British Isles. As the ice made its final retreat northward in approximately 7000 BC, Mesolithic foragers journeyed northward to access the green pastures it left in its wake. Little is known about the earliest of Scotland's inhabitants since they left little archaeological evidence behind.

A Greek mariner left behind the first written reference to Scotland in about 320 BC. Pytheas referred to the northern part of the British Isles with the name *Orcas*—a Celtic word that was most probably derived from the name of a local tribe he encountered during his travels. It means "the young boars" and lives on in modern times as Orkney, a rugged archipelago off Scotland's northeastern coast. It also provides evidence that Celtic speakers were present that far up north by fourth century BC.

The earliest extensive historical record dates to Rome's first encounter with medieval Scotland. The feared Roman legions arrived towards the end of the first century AD, after they successfully conquered the Celtic tribes of England and Wales after three decades of subjugation. Like their southern counterparts, the inhabitants of Scotland (or Caledonia, as the Romans referred to it then) mostly spoke a form of Celtic language. Unlike southern Britain, however, Caledonia's fierce warrior tribes would mount an effective resistance against the mighty Roman Empire.[6] Roman ambitions to access Scotland's lead, silver, and gold with plans to enrich itself further by enslaving the Scottish tribes and forcing them to pay taxes would eventually be thwarted.

By the time the Romans first encountered Scotland, a "chiefdom society" which was more hierarchical and unequal had emerged. Large underground stores (souterrains) were a contributor to this social inequality, allowing local chiefs to hoard surplus crops and resources they had extracted from the land. Hierarchies within Scottish settlements gave way to hierarchies between settlements, as tribes (which each consisted of a few thousand members) vied with each other for power and control over resources.[7]

In the presence of a foreign common enemy, the warring tribes united to defend their homeland. In 79 A.D, the Roman governor led the first incursion into Caledonia.[8] After a few campaigns, the Romans achieved a decisive victory in 83 A.D at the battle of Mons Graupius. General Julius Agricola defeated the Caledonians there (they were fighting under the leadership of Calgacus, a chieftain of the Caledonian Confederacy). When their initial vision of conquering the entire British Isles was finally at hand, however, the Roman military found that their attention was needed in other parts of their empire.

To safeguard Rome's glorious conquest of southern Britain against the fierce Scottish warriors, the Romans built Hadrian's Wall on the Tyne-Solway line in the 120s and 130s.[9] During the middle of the second century, a second wall (Antonine Wall) was built on the Forth-Clyde line.[10] This reoccupation only lasted for roughly a decade. After briefly including southern Scotland within the Roman province of Britannia, the Romans eventually gave up their campaign against tribes which were uncharitably described as the "barbarians from the north" and relatively idealized as "the last men on earth, the last of the free." They retreated to Hadrian's Wall. Roman presence was maintained in the southwest part of Scotland, near Hadrian's Wall, until the decline of the Roman Empire.

Despite Rome's aborted conquest of Scotland, its empire left behind a profound influence on the inhabitants of Caledonia. The duality was not entirely between the "imperial Roman" and the "oppressed Native," but between those who were within and outside the mighty empire. The inhabitants of the British Isles had the opportunity to join the Roman army for their own gain, while others undoubtedly saw the benefits of aligning themselves with the most extensive political and social entity in the west.

Like all imperial powers, Rome impacted the locals through a combination of hard and soft power. Apart from their military prowess, they came with Roman commodities, luxury items, and wealth that could be used to seduce local leaders to their cause. The rivaling warrior chiefs were thus incentivized to take advantage of Roman resources to gain a competitive edge over their rivals. When they came face-to-face with the various trade objects that circulated through Rome's international economic system, the Caledonians inevitably realized that they were isolated from an international highway of ideas, trade, and cultural exchange.

Rome's most lasting effect on the Caledonians is undoubtedly the introduction of Christianity. The religion of the empire slowly extended its influence up north, reaching places and communities that the Roman military would not. Much of the evangelizing work was probably done by British and Irish missionaries who were intent on converting the northern pagans to their cause. The new religion came with new trade links to the Irish Sea and Atlantic Gaul, which provided the foreign objects necessary for the new Christians to conduct their rituals of faith. These were pottery designed to contain wine and oil, which were inevitably accompanied by new aesthetic and intellectual conceptions.

Chapter 2 - Kenneth MacAlpin, King of the Picts

Five main languages were widely spoken in the territory that is now Scotland in the ninth century. These included three Celtic languages (Briton,[11] Pict,[12] and Gael/Scot[13]) and two Germanic languages (Angle[14] and Norse). It is a historical irony that the most widely spoken language at the time—Picts—was the only one that would eventually become extinct.

Britons and Picts might have a shared a common ancestor and originally shared a common language as well, but they began to diverge into two politically and culturally distinct communities by the eighth century. The term "Picti," which means "painted people," was first used by Roman writers as early as the late third century. They were described as enigmatic savage pagans, a tribe that refused to become Romanized or to embrace Christianity (as their southern counterparts did). Little remains of their civilization, but there is evidence to suggest that they were not simply primitive warriors. The Picts left behind archaeological evidence of their architecture, art, education, and religion.[15] They provided no written records for historians to study, but their sophisticated symbols, which can be found on various objects and upright stone monuments, gives off a hint of their burgeoning ethnic and political identity. The lack of any Roman alphabet amongst Pictish relics is especially telling.

The Roman presence intensified the rivalries between the different regional kingdoms vying for power across the land. The various Germanic tribes that had settled across eastern Britain were beginning to develop a sense of "Englishness," while their counterparts in the west were developing a sense of unity based on their mutual anti-Anglo-Saxon stance. Across the Irish Sea, the various Irish kingdoms were rallying around a shared "Gaelic" identity.[16] It is highly likely that the strong regional identities which had persevered throughout the north during the early medieval period were coalescing into a shared "Pictish" identity due to similar historical factors.

In 400 AD, the Romans made a complete withdrawal from the British Isles as their vaunted empire was increasingly threatened by European tribes. The power vacuum they left behind was soon claimed by the local tribes, who began to exert their control over larger swaths of territories. Despite the Roman exodus, Christianity remained and solidified its presence in Scotland. The kings of Dál Riata[17] (a Gaelic kingdom that extended from Northern Ireland to the west coast of modern Scotland) gave Saint Columba[18]—an Irish abbot and missionary who spread Catholicism across the northern British Isles—sufficient land to form a monastery in 565 AD. Iona thus emerged as an influential center for Christian learning and evangelism in the Celtic world across the next two centuries.[19]

The Picts nevertheless found themselves confronting another fearsome foreign force throughout the 9th century. The monasteries and the treasures they contained served as a magnet for the Vikings,[20] who sailed across the North Sea to terrorize their southern neighbors and to escape the overpopulation on Norway's west coast. The plunderers seized all the gold and silver (in the form of saintly relics and decorative metalwork) they could find and did not hesitate to murder anyone that stood in the way. Their violent raids eventually gave way to settlements, which allowed them to gain control over large areas of Scotland, Ireland, and England. By the middle of the 9th century, Norse settlements of the western and northern isles and of Caithness and Sutherland were well underway. The image of the peripatetic Viking warrior endures to the modern day, but the truth is that their most important reason for migration was to secure new lands for farming, craftwork, and trade.

The fearsome Viking invasions sowed the seeds of extinction for the once-powerful Pictish kingdoms. The Vikings destroyed a monastic settlement at Portmahomack in approximately 820, signaling a decisive change in the status quo. During this period of tumult and confusion, a heroic figure emerged to unite the land against their common seafaring foe.

Kenneth MacAlpin[21] was a Gaelic king who lost his father during an earlier battle with the once-powerful Pictish kingdom. MacAlpin took advantage of the crisis to unite the Gaels and Picts against their common foe. There is also evidence to suggest that his mother had been a Pictish princess; his mixed ancestry might have lent a helping hand to the cause (the Pictish were matrilineal, giving him a blood claim to both thrones). A common culture and political identity was thus forged by the shared need to defend the realm. MacAlpin consolidated his power across the realm by instilling obedience to a single king. As a result, the regional kingdoms across the land lost much of their powers. Instead of regional kings, they became officials who were known as mormaers, or "sea stewards". When the Vikings amassed a fleet of 140 ships to destroy and conquer Dál Riata at the beginning of the 9th century, however, the Gaelic kingdom was brought to an abrupt end. The Gaels relocated the relics of their saints to Pictland (in eastern Scotland), where their presence as Gaelic overlords earned them resentment from the Picts.[22]

The union between the Picts and Scots created Alba,[23] a unified kingdom that spanned across Argyll and Bute to Caithness and included a large majority of central and southern Scotland. Under MacAlpin's leadership, Alba managed to defend itself against the relentless Viking invasions. Despite this victory, the Picts probably had mixed feelings about the new status quo. Gaelic influence, Gaelic Christianity, and Gaelic traditions spread across the formerly Pictish lands with a greater intensity than ever before. The spread of culture probably occurred in both ways, as the Gaels intermarried with the Picts and adopted some of their manners and customs. By 839 A.D, the Pictish kingdom had been practically annihilated by the Vikings.

When MacAlpin died in 858, his political and historical legacy was clear. The Pictish and Gaelic kingdoms had merged with each other and evolved into the new Kingdom of Alba. Dál Riata disappeared from the chronicles, as did the Picts. The foundation for a Scottish kingdom had been laid down. At his funeral, Gaelic bards mourned his passing: "That Kenneth with his host is no more brings weeping to every home. No king of his worth under heaven is there, to the bounds of Rome."

Chapter 3: Macbeth, the Regicidal King

Macduff: Stands Scotland where it did?
Ross: Alas, poor country! Almost afraid to know itself.

Macbeth, William Shakespeare[24]

The Tragedy of Macbeth[25] stands alongside *Hamlet*, *King Lear*, and *Julius Caesar* as one of William Shakespeare's most enduring tragedies. The play was written sometime between 1604 and 1606, over five centuries since the real Scottish king it was based on, Mac Bethad mac Findláich, or Macbeth,[26] was buried. With its prophetic witches, regicide, apparitions of guilt, and a ruthless leading female protagonist (Lady Macbeth), *The Tragedy of Macbeth* has certainly earned a place in literary history.

Despite its iconic fame, however, Shakespeare's play was far from historical truth.[27] The legendary English poet and playwright used the Holinshed's *Chronicles of England, Scotland and Ireland* (1587) as the primary source for his plot, which were itself riddled in inaccuracies. He also tailored it to fit the tastes of the new reigning English king of his time, King James I. James I had a well-documented interest in witches, witchcraft, and the supernatural—hence the play's opening scene where the Three Witches encounter Macbeth and his friend Banquo. There are various discrepancies between the play and documented historical fact, but modern viewers should especially take note of the fact that Shakespeare took a great liberty with the timeline. While the events in the play unfold over the course of a single year, Macbeth remained on the throne of Alba (Scotland did not exist yet) for 17 years.

The well-known murder did happen, but not in the way Shakespeare narrated it. Before he assumed the throne, Macbeth succeeded his father Findlaech as the chief (or mormaer) of the province of Moray in northern Scotland in 1031. Historians believe that he might have been a grandson of King Kenneth II (reigned 971–995). He married

Gruoch (i.e., Lady Macbeth), who was a descendant of King Kenneth III (reigned 997–1005).

Shakespeare paints Macbeth and his wife as ruthless and immoral in their pursuit of political power, but the realities of history are far more complex. Duncan I[28] was the king of Alba from 1034 to 1040 and had inherited the kingship from his grandfather King Malcolm II[29] (who reigned from 1005–1034), who had himself betrayed the established system of royal succession in Alba. The kingship was supposed to be alternated between two different branches of the royal family—a tradition that gave his cousin Macbeth a better claim to the throne.

The rivalry between the two cousins who each had a rightful claim to the throne through their mothers culminated in Duncan's unsuccessful attempt to besiege Durham. The following year, Macbeth murdered him during a battle at Elgin (and not on his bed as he slept, as in Shakespeare's version of events). Macbeth proved to be a respected and wise king who lived on to rule Alba for 17 years. Apart from enforcing law and order across the land, he encouraged his people to embrace Christianity. In 1050, conditions in Alba were peaceful and secure enough for him to embark on a pilgrimage to Rome.[30] Unfortunately for him, however, history was destined to repeat itself. Duncan's son Malcolm Canmore[31] had escaped to Northumbria after his father was defeated and had never intended to give up his claim to the throne. In 1054, his uncle Siward, Earl of Northumbria, challenged Macbeth for the throne on behalf of his nephew. His army defeated Macbeth's at the Battle of Dunsinnan. Macbeth kept the throne but agreed to restore Malcolm's lands to him. Three years later, Malcolm defeated and killed him at the Battle of Lumphanan in Aberdeenshire—this time with help from the English.

Macbeth's life story demonstrates the fragility of medieval kingship throughout this era. A kingship could only be sustained if the king could maintain his political dominance against all his rivals. The system of succession in Alba was tanistry[32] (which is of Celtic origins), which allows a king to be succeeded by any man who had a grandfather who once held the kingship. A man could also lay claim to the throne through a royal mother. When they were multiple claimants (as was often the case), a closer link was advantageous. A council of elders would then collectively decide on which candidate had the strongest claim to the throne. Other attributes (age, wealth, military skill, and personal qualities) were also taken into account. While some early Scottish kings held on to the kingship for decades and died peacefully, many met violent and abrupt ends due to a royal power struggle. Power was thus often secured through the murder of one's predecessor. The contest for kingship largely depended on one's royal standing, access to resources and supporters, and personal ability, rather than ethnicity alone.

Over the years, the northern chiefdom societies evolved to accommodate more intricate structures of government. There was little bureaucracy at this point, but kings began to oversee the law, order, and justice across their lands. With the help of local lords, officials, and legal specialists, they arbitrated disputes and introduced new laws when necessary. Diplomacy was also a crucial concern, as alliances between territories were seldom stable.

Macbeth's embrace and promotion of Christianity also point towards the emerging ideology of a Christian kingship[33] in the north. It was no longer sufficient for a king to maintain his standing through the use of armed followers and the control of fortified castles and fortresses. Kings began spending more time at the most influential monasteries, solidifying the interdependence between the once-secular elite classes and the Church. They celebrated major Christian rituals at monasteries they favored and invited leading clerics to participate in crucial royal ceremonies. Both parties were invested in maintaining stability, peace, and a strong leadership that could stand the test of time.

Chapter 4 – The Emergence of the Scottish Nation-State

During Macbeth's relatively long and peaceful reign, southerners who were loyal to him migrated northwards, opting to resettle in the southwest and northeast of modern-day Scotland. They brought with them a more international outlook and culture, sowing the seeds of foreign influence in a predominantly Gaelic society. Gaelic traditions and customs prevailed in everyday life, the Church, and the royal courts, as well as the institutions of law and education. This was set to change throughout the eleventh and twelfth centuries.

The rising presence of foreign influence in the north can be traced back to Malcolm Canmore who became the king of Alba as Malcolm III in 1058 (after Macbeth's death the previous year). His first wife, Ingibjorg, had been the daughter of a Norse earl of Orkney, but his second wife, Margaret,[34] was a descendant of England's Saxon royal house. As a queen consort and patroness of the church, Margaret ushered in a climate of receptiveness to southern cultural influences (i.e., the Anglicization of Scotland). By influencing her husband and his court, she advanced the causes of the Gregorian reform (which was mainly preoccupied with the clergy's independence from the state) and the conquered English population. Margaret also relocated Benedictine monks from Canterbury, England, to her new foundation at Dunfermline, establishing the precedent for non-Gaelic-speaking clergymen to influence Scottish culture.

When Malcolm III died during his final English raid in 1093, however, there were concerted attempts to prevent the replacement of tanistry with primogeniture.[35] This southern custom privileged the legitimate firstborn son above everyone else (younger brothers, older or younger illegitimate sons, and collateral relatives) when it came to inheriting his parent's throne, estate, or wealth. Under tanistry, the heir to the king *could* be the eldest son, but this was not necessarily the case. A council of family heads could opt to elect a brother, nephew, or cousin of the previous chieftain—anyone who was linked by blood and deemed most worthy of the position.

Malcolm III's brother and son (from his first marriage) each briefly occupied the throne after his death. In time, however, it was Malcolm III's three sons, with the assistance of Margaret, who secured their control over the throne. Edgar was king from 1097–1107, followed by Alexander I (1107–24), and David I (1124–53). With the help of the English, they defied Celtic opposition and claims from the descendants of their father's first marriage. Their rise to power was accompanied by the increasing practice of primogeniture, which

finally replaced tanistry permanently during the late 13th century.

The presence of Latin in Scotland had linked it to the international culture of the Christian Church over the previous decades, which paved the way for the impact of other influences from continental Europe. Throughout the twelfth and thirteenth centuries, the "Europeanization of Europe" was underway, as the modern Western European state began developing in England, France, Norway, and Germany. They were categorized by clearly-defined borders, national sovereignty, a commercial economy, parliamentary representation, thoroughly institutionalized administrative and legal systems, and a shared idea of nationhood. The arrival of immigrants from Normandy, Brittany, and Flanders accelerated the disruption of Gaelic norms and traditions, bringing in new influences, ideas, and practices that could be repurposed for Scottish ends.

David I,[36] the youngest of Malcolm III's six sons with Margaret, played a major role in Scotland's evolution into a modern nation-state. He eventually proved himself to be one of the most powerful and influential Scottish kings. Unlike his mother who did not interfere much with the inner workings of the Church, he actively reorganized Scottish Christianity to align it with its counterparts in England and continental Europe. This meant that there was a clear division between the secular and regular clergy, as well as a complete system of parishes and dioceses. He also founded several religious communities, mainly for Cistercian monks and Augustinian canons. On the political front, David I introduced an Anglo-French (Norman) aristocracy that would go on to play a significant role in Scottish history.[37] Much of his early life had been spent at the court of his brother-in-law, King Henry I of England. Like his father before him, his marriage to a prominent Englishwoman (a daughter of Waltheof, earl of Northumbria) earned him significant political clout in England. Through his wife, he became the earl of Huntingdon, a title that came with large swaths of land in Northamptonshire. His Anglo-Norman[38] connections helped him secure the right to rule Cumbria, Strathclyde, and part of Lothian before he succeeded the throne from his older brother Alexander I.

Despite his English connections, David I remained an independent king who was intent on drawing from English culture and bureaucracy to empower Scotland.[39] He paved the way for the arrival of other Anglo-Norman families to migrate northward by providing generous rewards of offices and lands. These included the Bruces in Annandale, the Fitzalans of Arundel, and the de Morvilles in Ayrshire. They were given control of large estates in peripheral areas where David I's regal authority could not be easily enforced.

This decentralized form of government thus introduced a form of feudalism[40] in Scotland. A four tier-hierarchy developed, with the king at the apex followed by the nobles, knights, and serfs. The nobles possessed lands from the Crown for their military services, which were provided through the training and recruitment of knights. These knights also protected the peasants on their lord's lands, who provided their labor and a share of their crops in exchange for this protection. Similar feudal arrangements had existed amongst the clan systems of the Scottish Highlands, but these were mainly based on family bonds instead of written charters and legal contracts.

David I's rule over the Scottish kingdom was also consolidated through the creation of a more sophisticated government administration. He introduced the office of sheriff (vicecomes), a royal judge, and an administrator for each area of the kingdom (who was based within a royal castle). Central government officials such as the chancellor, the chamberlain, and the justiciar were introduced to the royal court. The royal court began playing the role of supreme court of law and parliament, maintaining an efficient government that facilitated peace and the flourishing of a medieval economy and society.

There are four main characteristics which clearly differentiated David I's kingship from the traditional Celtic-style kingship that his predecessors had practiced.[41] Firstly, he extended royal power into practically every aspect of life (mainly the religious and the economic). He reformed the Scottish Church and extended its religious orders across the land, while also introducing an English-type market economy. This included the introduction of formal markets and fairs that required trading licenses that were administered by the crown. He minted the first Scottish coinage and founded the kingdom's four royal burghs (Berwick, Edinburgh, Perth, and Aberdeen). His trusted nobles established firm local lordships centered on well-defended castles. They also sent their knights to serve in his army, which allowed him to experiment with the various tools and policies of an English-style administrative kingship.

Secondly, he established a more totalizing and monopolistic royal lordship across a "greater Scotland"—a tradition that greatly benefited his successors. The older tradition of tanistry—which nearly always engendered great chaos and uncertainty—was abandoned in favor of a stricter order for royal succession. This left the regional kings with little opportunity to compete for the throne; succession was now a matter of direct lineage. True to his centralizing ambitions, David preemptively elected his only son Henry as a co-ruler in 1135. After Henry's unexpected early demise in 1152, David appointed his oldest grandson as his apparent heir.

Malcolm IV[42] thus became king in 1153 at the previously implausible age of 12 when his grandfather died (a regent nevertheless safeguarded the throne until he was old enough to rule on his own). A strict adherence to primogeniture thus helped to spare the Scottish kingdom from disruptive upheavals and violent competition for the throne.

Thirdly, David I and his government sought to empower the Scottish kingship to be on equal footing with the English kingship. The objective was to thwart the English monarchy's imperial aspirations and to foster a greater sense of identity and status as a decidedly independent kingdom. The Scottish Church thus lobbied the Pope for papal approval of the Scottish kingship, an effort that was thwarted until 1329 by rigorous English lobbying. This concept of a "divine" and "semi-sacred" kingship was also a potent means for David I to consolidate his rule. In the meantime, the Scottish Church insisted on remaining independent from the influence of its counterparts in Canterbury or York.

Finally, the Scottish kings began to seek a stronger footing on an international stage. They embraced European courtly fashions and began participating in international diplomacy. David I succeeded in winning respect and admiration from his continental European peers —the first Scottish monarch to do so. He even envisioned himself as a potential leader of the Second Crusade. His court embraced English and French (which were both the lingua franca of political society) to such an extent that an Englishman commented that the Scots "regarded themselves as... Frenchmen in race, manners, language, and culture."[43] Scottish princesses began marrying continental princes with greater frequency, while their male counterparts married English, French, and Norwegian princesses or high-born women. From here on, the Scottish kings insisted on being viewed as equals to the Western European monarchs.

Chapter 5 – The Golden Age

David I's modernizing reign lasted for nearly three decades, from 1124 to 1153. By the time he died and was replaced by his grandson Malcolm IV, his lands had sprawled forth to include Newcastle and Carlisle. His wealth and power rivaled the king of England, which undoubtedly helped him to maintain his mythical status as a saintly and powerful ruler throughout the land. The Scottish kings who followed suit may not have matched the immensity of his achievements, but they built on his legacy in their own ways. The inhabitants of Scotland thus enjoyed an unprecedented period of prolonged peace and prosperity from David I (reigned 1124–1153) to Alexander III (reigned 1249–1286).

The Scottish economy flourished for over a century due to innovation and progress. A predominantly agrarian economy gave way to urbanization, where the burghs (incorporated towns) bustled as hubs for trade and small-scale manufacturing. David I helped facilitate the evolution of towns in Edinburgh, Dunfermline, Perth, Stirling, Inverness, and Aberdeen by encouraging intranational and international trade, introducing a robust legal system, and providing security against attacks from pirates and mercenaries. Each burgh was also allowed to develop their own laws to regulate trading transactions and resolve disputes. If a local burgh was unable to resolve a dispute, it could be referred to the Court of the Four Burghs (which initially included Berwick, Edinburgh, Roxburgh, and Stirling).

Berwick[44] may not rival the international reputations of Glasgow[45] and Edinburgh[46] (the state capital, now and then) today, but it was *the* epicenter for Scottish economic activity during this time. Despite David I's English ties, Scotland counted northern Germany and Scandinavia as its primary trading partners during the 12th and 13th centuries. Despite being home to only half a million people (for comparison, England had approximately 2 million people), Scottish farmers produced more wool and cattle than their English counterparts. They also had the benefit of low taxation, access to ample amounts of food and wine, and the luxury of plying their trade along a good transportation network. Many of the original townspeople were actually relative newcomers to Scotland, eager for a chance to focus on their economic activities instead of struggling to survive in locales plagued by territorial disputes and never-ending medieval warfare.

Medieval visitors to Berwick compared it to Alexandria for its wealth and sizable population. The stereotypes of the Scots as a barbaric and tribal people was not evident here. Indeed, Berwick's annual customs revenue alone was estimated to amount to twenty-five percent of England's as a whole. The presence of well-endowed monasteries, stately abbeys, and grand churches reflected the strong and genteel influence of Christianity over all aspects of life. Its presence as a unifying religion undoubtedly helped to maintain the peace and harmony between the multicultural communities that lived in close proximity to one another. Political conflicts often disrupted the general peace and stability that David I's successors enjoyed, but it did not have a major impact on the economy. David I's grandson Malcolm IV did not match his cult of personality or reputation, but he was nevertheless a relatively successful king. He never married and had a reputation for chastity (this earned him the unflattering nickname "the Maiden"). He did decide to surrender Cumbria and Northumbria to Henry II to build better relations with

England, but he also was successful in defeating Somerled.[47] Somerled was a powerful "King of the Isles," a regional ruler that reigned in the Western Isles of Scotland that were primarily allied to the Norwegian kingdom. He had ambitions to make the islands an entirely independent kingdom and was victorious against the Scandinavians in Argyll. His aim to include parts of the mainland into his territory ultimately sealed his violent death at the hands of his own nephew, William I.

William I[48] succeeded Malcolm IV in 1165 and shared David I's expansionist objectives. He earned the nickname "William the Lion" for successfully subduing the north (across the Moray Firth) and building royal castles there. His plans to reclaim Northumbria from the English unfortunately resulted in humiliation. During a failed raid into England, he was captured by Henry II's men. In exchange for his release, he and other Scottish nobles agreed to acknowledge Henry II as their feudal overlord via the Treaty of Falaise (1174). As a result, English garrisons were placed all over Scotland. William was able to redeem himself in 1189, when he negotiated for the Treaty of Falaise to be annulled in exchange for a hefty payment of 10,000 marks via the Quitclaim of Canterbury (1189).

English kings could nevertheless still advance more ambiguous claims of superiority over Scotland, as they had throughout the previous century. Thankfully, William the Lion's successors were competent kings who succeeded in maintaining the peace, power, and prosperity that David I had attained. William's son Alexander II[49] (reigned 1214–1249) secured a lasting peace between Scotland and England with the Anglo-Scottish agreement of 1217. This mutual commitment was strengthened by his marriage to Henry III's sister Joan in 1221. This meant that the longstanding ambition to claim Northumbria as part of Scotland had to be renounced, however. The border between England and Scotland was thus established by the Tweed-Solway line after centuries of indeterminacy.

Alexander III[50] (reigned 1249–1286) followed his father's choice of a politically strategic marriage. In 1251, he married Henry III's daughter Margaret. He proved to be a wise and beloved king who expanded the kingdom with the acquisition of the western Highlands and Isles after the Battle of Largs (which is also known as the Last Battle of the Vikings) in 1263.[51] King Haakon Haakonsson's catastrophic defeat marked the end of Viking influence over

Scotland.[52] When Alexander III met an abrupt and unexpected end in 1286, however, the integrity of his own kingdom was severely threatened. With his death, Scotland's long and cherished golden age came to an end.

Chapter 6 – The Wars of Independence

Alexander III's two sons had died before him in 1281 and 1284. In hopes of a male heir, he had recently married a young French noblewoman, Joleta of Dreux. (His first wife, Princess Margaret of England had died in 1275.) Despite a dire prophecy of his impending doom by Thomas the Rhymer, the famous prophet, he decided to ride home to his castle at night during a treacherous storm. After losing contact with his guides and esquire, he and his horse were found dead at the bottom of a cliff the next morning.

All hope was technically not lost, as Alexander III had arranged for his young granddaughter Margaret[53] (the "Maid of Norway") to assume the Scottish throne. The appointed guardians of Scotland arranged for her hand in marriage with Lord Edward (King Edward I's then-five-year-old son) via the Treaty of Birgham[54] (1290) in hopes of maintaining the peace between Scotland and England. When Margaret died due to seasickness while sailing from Norway to Scotland four years later, however, the longstanding Scottish monarchy had come to an untimely end.

After Margaret's death, no less than 13 claimants for the Scottish crown revealed their plans for the throne. The majority of these were Scottish magnates. The guardians made the costly mistake of inviting Edward I to serve as an external arbitrator for these claims. Edward I, who had already proven his appetite and aptitude for expansion and conquest with the dominion of Ireland and Wales, did not waste any time in making full use of the power void. Instead of being an impartial judge, he opted to assert his position as Scotland's feudal superior. The claimants to the throne were in a poor position to oppose Edward I, as were the various members of the Scottish nobility who held precious land titles in England.

The common people of Scotland (i.e., the "community of the realm") and the Scottish clergy were nevertheless deeply opposed to the idea of an English dominion. Edward I's heavy-handed attempt to assimilate Scotland into England ultimately prompted the rise of a powerful sense of national unity that rose from the grassroots to the upper echelons of the Scottish social hierarchy. Their antagonism to English presence in everyday life and through unwanted interference from the English Church would engender a nationalism that cut across barriers of region, class, ethnicity, and language. This hard-won national consciousness certainly did not emerge overnight. Edward I was initially able to extend his dominion over Scotland—maintaining it was what ultimately proved to be untenable.

The two main candidates for the throne were John de Balliol[55] and Robert de Bruce.[56] Both men had many supporters and armed forces at their command. Edward I had a logical reason to choose John Balliol over Robert Bruce, but it was also in his favor that the former possessed large swaths of land in northern England. He had far more to lose if he chose to defy his self-appointed English overlord.

Balliol did endure a series of humiliations as Edward I unsubtly exerted his overlordship. He made every Scottish magnate, knight, freeman, and religious leader swear their loyalty to him (as Lord Paramount of Scotland) or risk harsh penalties. Edward also made Balliol repeat his homage to him multiple times in front of all the other Scottish nobles. Balliol's resentment at being blatantly reduced to a puppet figure grew. When Edward took it a step further to have English judges preside over law cases that were being appealed in Scottish courts and demanded that Balliol send his knights to perform military service for the English war with France, a full-fledged rebellion was sparked.

In 1295, the Scottish established an alliance with France in their opposition to England. The historic Auld Alliance was primarily motivated by Scotland and France's mutual interest in curtailing England's expansionary ambitions. While it was primarily intended to be a military and diplomatic alliance, it also had long-lasting cultural effects on Scotland. It granted Scottish merchants the opportunity to gain first choice in importing Bordeaux's finest wines – a privilege that the Scots held on to for centuries. Scottish appetites for French wines persisted even in the face of the Reformation, which created an irreconcilable rift between Catholic France and Protestant Scotland.

In response to Scotland's rekindled alliance with France, Edward I ordered his army to annihilate Berwick. He also ordered for all of Balliol's English titles and properties to be confiscated. His army of three thousand foot soldiers and five thousand horsemen wreaked havoc on Scotland's prized city to deter the Scottish resistance. Out of a population of approximately twenty thousand people, only three thousand survived the massacre and pillage. The Scottish persevered, but they were no match for the most sophisticated military force in all of Europe. Edward I eventually captured no less than 130 high-ranking Scottish knights, as well as several earls and prominent magnates. After he seized control of all major Scottish castles—Roxburgh Castle, Edinburgh Castle, and Stirling Castle—there was no option but to surrender.

Balliol was shipped off to England and placed on an indeterminate house arrest. The Scottish nobility had lost their will to resist English subjugation by now, leaving William Wallace[57]—a knight's son with no lands or prestige to his name—to emerge as an iconic embodiment of the Scottish desire for independence. After a series of skirmishes against the obnoxious English knights and officials that made life difficult for the Scottish common people, Wallace evolved from a rebel outlaw into an ingenious guerrilla leader.

Tales of his heroic exploits (which mirrored the English legend of Robin Hood) and his ascendance to near-mythical status (a Christ-like resurrection from the dead and a prophecy of national heroism) attracted followers and allies across the land. In 1297, Wallace made full use of an advantageous terrain and English military overconfidence to land an astounding victory at the Battle of Stirling Bridge. This was Scotland's most significant victory against the English army since the Dark Ages. Wallace's newfound power and fame as a national hero and military genius was nevertheless short-lived. During the Battle of Falkirk[58] the following year, he suffered from a devastating defeat. He died via a gory execution in London in 1305, partly because his lowly social status had triggered envy, resentment, and opposition from many members of the Scottish nobility. Without their united support, Wallace's army of rebels could not hold out against Edward I's military might for long.

Wallace's excruciating death was not in vain. In his place, a royal rebel rose to forcefully unite the Scottish nobility to resist the "hammer of the Scots." The eighth Robert de Bruce, the grandson of Balliol's main competitor for the throne, ultimately staged an unexpected revolt in 1306. Like Wallace before him, Bruce realized that his only opportunity to best the more numerous and technologically advanced English army was by relying on ambushes, guerrilla tactics, surprise attacks, and unconventional military strategies.[59] After suffering from a series of agonizing defeats (and enduring the executions of many of his family members), Bruce turned the tables and achieved a series of career-making victories against the English: the Battle of Glen Trool[60] in 1307, the Battle of Loudoun Hill[61] that same year, and the historic Battle of Bannockburn[62] in 1314 (where his men defeated the largest English army to ever invade Scotland).

Robert the Bruce proved himself as a skillful statesman and military leader, excelling both at harrying Edward I's attempts to subjugate him and at firmly suppressing his local opponents. When Edward I finally died in 1307—while journeying to the Scottish frontlines, no less—Bruce was able to take advantage of his successor Edward II's weaknesses to negotiate for Scottish independence.

In 1320, he put forth the Declaration of Arbroath with the help of his advisers. It was framed as a letter from the Scottish magnates to the Pope, announcing their allegiance to Bruce as the rightful king of Scotland. It also sought the Roman Church's support for Scotland as an independent kingdom from England and to reverse the Pope's excommunication of Bruce (he had risen to power by murdering a rival for the throne in a church). In October 1328, Pope John XXII finally lifted Bruce's excommunication.

It was Edward II's hopeless incompetence and local enemies that eventually helped Bruce secure an English recognition of Scotland's independence. Edward II was deposed from power by his own wife, Princess Isabella of France, with the help of her lover, exiled English baron Roger Mortimer. She replaced him with their young son Edward III, who was in a highly vulnerable position and ill-equipped to maintain a war against Scotland while also having to suppress the rebellious English nobles.

The Treaty of Edinburgh-Northampton[63] was signed by Edward III (under pressure from his mother and Mortimer) and Bruce in 1328. It dictated that he renounced all claims of overlordship over the kingdom of Scotland, sought to maintain the peace between the two kingdoms via the arranged marriage between Bruce's son David and Edward III's sister Joan, and officially recognized Bruce as the rightful king of the Scots. Bruce himself died the following year, having sealed his place in Scottish history. The traditions that had been established during the long and torturous Wars of Independence—to pursue self-sufficiency despite the high costs incurred and to turn towards continental Europe for inspiration and alliances—would persist until the 16th century.

Both William Wallace and Robert Bruce enjoy a seemingly immortal place in the hearts and minds of subsequent generations of Scottish men and women. Wallace's status as a patriot of the first order endures via an epic poem by fifteenth-century Scottish royal court poet Harry the Minstrel (or "Blind Harry").[64] *The Actes and Deidis of the Illustre and Vallyeant Campioun Schir William Wallace* (Acts and Deeds of the Illustrious and Valiant Champion Sir William Wallace, a.k.a. *The Wallace*) enshrined Wallace's mythical status over the centuries, which then reached a global audience via Mel Gibson's 1995 blockbuster Oscar-winning film *Braveheart*.[65] Bruce is less well-known outside of Scotland, but his contributions to the nation are similarly preserved for posterity via John Barbour's[66] 14th-century poem *The Bruce*—the first major work of Scottish literature.

Chapter 7 – The Black Death

Historians tend to foreground human actions and consequences when attempting to reconstruct the past. The pages of history are filled with the lives of kings, popes, powerful human institutions, wars, battles, and periods of significant cultural change like the Reformation and Industrial Revolution. Numbers tend to be freer from such biases. The Scottish casualties from the many battles and skirmishes with the English military throughout the Scottish wars of independence were certainly significant. However, the catastrophic impact of The Black Death on Scotland cannot be ignored.[67]

After killing millions as it spread westward from China and throughout the Mediterranean, the Black Death devastated England between 1348 and 1349. Deaths were caused by a combination of fatal airborne diseases: the bubonic plague (during the summer months), the pneumonic plague (during winter), and possibly anthrax. Modern scientific studies attribute the infection to the bacterium *Yersinia pestis* (this strain is ancestral to all currently existing *Y. pestis* strains), but there is also evidence to indicate that it may have had viral origins. The inhabitants of medieval Europe believed that the plague was airborne, but scientists believe that it actually spread on the backs of rodents (primarily rats) who were surreptitiously infested with plague-carrying fleas.

London was hit in September 1348, with the entirety of East Anglia affected the following year. Wales and the Midlands were infected by the spring of 1349. That summer, it spread across the Irish Sea and penetrated northward into Scotland. Historians believe that the Scots had been infected because they chose to attack various English towns as they were succumbing to the plague. Believing that the disease was retribution from God, nearly five thousand Scottish soldiers fielded a botched attempt to invade England.

Scotland did not suffer as much as its Western European counterparts because of its cooler climate and more dispersed population. Even so, the plague was capable of wiping out the majority of the urban populations based in cities like Glasgow and Edinburgh. An English account of the pandemic reveals that even small villages were not fully spared from its deadly embrace:

> Sometimes it came by road, passing from village to village, sometimes by river, as in the East Midlands, or by ship, from the Low Countries or from other infected areas. On the vills of the bishop of Worcester's estates in the West Midlands, they (the death rates) ranged between 19 per cent of manorial tenants at Hartlebury and Hanbury to no less than 80 per cent at Aston.... It is very difficult for us to imagine the impact of plague on these small rural communities, where a village might have no more than 400 or 500 inhabitants. Few settlements were totally depopulated, but in most others whole families must have been wiped out, and few can have been spared some loss, since the plague killed indiscriminately, striking at rich and poor alike.

"The World Upside Down," in *Black Death in England*, J. Bolton[68] Apart from the mystery of its origins and how it spread, the Black Death was so terrifying because of the speed in which it struck and the scale of its activity. Entire villages could be wiped out in a matter of days, while large urban areas could easily lose between eighty to ninety percent of their populations. The exact number of Scottish people that died due to the plague is unknown, but historians estimate that about a fifth of Scotland's population was lost during this time (approximately one million people). Even this conservative estimate is enough to make it the most fatal calamity in the history of the kingdom.[69] The very small minority who survived an infection had to live the rest of their lives with crippling mental and physical disabilities.

The first signs that someone had been infected was usually the emergence of lumps in the armpits or groins. After that, angry black spots began to appear on the thighs, arms, and other parts of the body. This was typically a death sentence within three days. The colder Scottish climate deterred the bubonic form of the plague, but it allowed the pneumonic, or septicaemic, plague to achieve a high death toll. The nobles were often spared by virtue of their isolation in the castles, but the middle and lower classes were mostly unable to escape its ravages.

To make matter worse, the plague was not a one-off phenomenon. Instead, it returned to haunt Scotland multiple times throughout the subsequent centuries (the final outbreak occurred in the 1640s). It stifled all aspects of life, from the economic to the political to the cultural. Children whose parents were dying from the plague refused to visit their deathbeds out of fear of becoming infected themselves. There was a shortage of labor, leaving many farms unmanned for years. Many fields were allowed to rot, reversing all the agricultural and manufacturing progress that had been achieved after the Wars of Independence finally came to an end. Wars were halted, as were much of intranational and international trade.

Combating the plague certainly took its toll on Scotland. In the 17th century, it finally managed to return to pre-plague population levels. This was achieved by the implementation of strict health controls whenever an outbreak occurred. People were prohibited from gathering and those believed to be infected were placed in quarantine. The Foul Clengers were widely employed in Edinburgh and other Scottish towns by this time. Their job was to relocate plague victims far away from human settlements to die and to burn all their homes, clothes, and possessions to the ground.

Chapter 8 – The House of Stewart

The Scottish economy recovered from the massive outbreak of plague by the 1370s. The exports of wool reached new heights, providing ample profits that ensured that the Scottish survivors of the plague had access to plenty of meat. This newfound prosperity also coincided with a new political development.

David II[70] had succeeded his father Robert the Bruce in 1329 when he was only five years old. By the time of David's death in 1371, Scotland had maintained the independence his father had fought so valiantly for. Like his father, he had been fairly successful in suppressing local opposition to his throne. The main threats to his power came from competing claims for the throne from John Balliol's descendants and hostility from the "disinherited" landowners who had been stripped of their titles by his father for supporting the English during the wars for independence. The war with England had been replaced by trade, allowing his citizens to enjoy the peace while his government used the taxes they collected to rebuild the kingdom. These taxes were also used to pay David II's ransom to England (100,000 marks), which had been incurred after he was captured during his attempt to invade England in 1346.

When he died unexpectedly, David II had been in the process of divorcing his second wife to marry his most recent mistress. This personal tumult was undoubtedly motivated by the urgency to produce an heir. David II had hoped for Edward III of England or one of his sons to assume the throne after he died, but this was an abominable prospect to the community of the realm who had endured years of hardship to retain their independence.

David II's manner of kingship and the Bruce dynasty were thus effectively buried with him. An entirely new dynasty emerged to fill the void—the House of Stewart[71] (which is also spelled as "Stuart" and "Steuart." David II was succeeded by Robert II,[72] who had been serving as the high steward of Scotland during David II's prolonged captivity. He was the son of Marjory (Robert Bruce's daughter) and Walter the Steward. Robert II was a fairly ineffectual and incompetent ruler, but he was an overachiever in the one domain that the Bruces had failed at. He fathered at least 21 children (with two wives and several mistresses) within his lifetime.

This surprisingly large number of offspring points towards Stewart's new model of kingship. Instead of a lone monarch exerting his power throughout the realm, Robert II was intent on elevating the size, status, and reach of his entire familial network. He married off his daughters to the lord of the Isles, the earl of Douglas, and other Scottish magnates. His sons were responsible for no less than eight earldoms and the duties of principal lieutenants. He bequeathed extended family members with patronage and empowered them to oversee distant regions.

This dynastic model of kingship had its advantages and disadvantages. On one hand, the sharing and spreading of power helped maintain political stability. When members of the royal family began competing overtly for power, however, that stability proved to be highly fragile. Bitter family feuds reared their ugly heads as Robert II was removed from active rule by his own son, the earl of Carrick. In 1388, he himself was ousted from his self-assumed lieutenant position by his younger brother, Robert of Fife.

These events were a precedent for a new development: the king could be stripped of his duties in favor of lieutenants who had wider support. After over a hundred years of continuous monarchical rule since before 1286, active kingship became an increasingly rare phenomenon. The kings from the House of Stewart were largely ineffectual and unreliable, leaving their lieutenants to assume control over important matters like war and justice. Guardians and governors also began to enjoy a newfound significance.

The Stewart kings were not without their own accomplishments, but they failed to rival the glory of a previous generation of monarchs. In one way or another, they left behind a legacy that left something to be desired: (1) Robert III[73] (reigned 1390-1406) was unable to prevent the English from capturing his own son; (2) James I[74] (reigned 1406–1437) spent most of his time as king raising taxes and confiscating lands from the Scottish nobility to pay off his English ransom; (3) James II[75] (reigned 1437–1460) assumed the throne after his father was murdered and assumed a penchant for warfare—he was killed by his own siege gun while besieging Roxburgh Castle; (4) James III[76] (reigned 1460–1488) was killed while attempting to escape the Battle of Sauchieburn in Stirlingshire. The weakness of the crown thus encouraged a more regionalized form of politics to take shape. Despite the king's reduced status and the limited influence of the royal government, the idea of a unified Scottish realm persisted. The king's symbolic power increased as his actual power diminished, partly due to epic poems like John Barbour's *The Bruce*, which signaled the emergence of a national body of literature. The Scottish Church and institutions of learning (e.g., the newly founded University of St. Andrews) also helped to ensure that the idea of an independent Scotland remained viable and attractive to all its inhabitants.

Founded in 1413, the University of St. Andrews was Scotland's first university and an entirely necessary development since Scotland could no longer send its students (who were often studying to become part of the clergy) to Paris. The Wars of Independence had prompted them to study in Paris, instead of Cambridge or Oxford.

When Scotland opted to recognize the antipope Benedict XIII[77] after France abandoned him, a local alternative was needed. The Great Western Schism (1378 – 1417) – which involved intense internal divisions caused by the advent of three rival popes within the Roman Catholic Church – thus played an unintended role of catalyzing the birth of Scotland's own institutions of higher education.[78] In 1451, Bishop William Turnbull founded the University of Glasgow,[79] Scotland's second university.

Chapter 9 – Mary, Queen of Scots: "The Daughter of Debate"

After a series of lackluster Stewart kingships, James IV[80] assumed the throne as a 15-year-old in 1488. Despite his young age, he proved to be adept at matters of war, politics, and culture. His primary achievements include the downfall of the last lord of the Isles, the founding of King's College (Scotland's third university) and improvements in education, and the great age of Scottish poetry. He also resolved the unrest along the Anglo-Scottish border and achieved a "treaty of perpetual peace" with England, which was sealed through his marriage with Henry VII's daughter Margaret Tudor in 1503.

Unfortunately, this peace proved to be far from perpetual. Henry VIII became complicit in Pope Julius II's anti-French campaign during the Italian Wars (1494 – 1559), prompting Scotland to renew its anti-England alliance with France.[81] During this time, the French king Charles VIII made several attempts to invade Italy with the help of Spain. To defend Rome, the papacy formed an alliance with Henry VIII, Venice and Florence in 1526. James IV responded to Henry VIII's French invasion by mounting a rash offensive against England. After successfully capturing four castles in northern England in August 1513, he suffered from a calamitous defeat. He perished, along with thousands of Scottish soldiers, at the disastrous Battle of Flodden.

His successor James V[82] (1513–42) worked to offset the extravagant costs of his predecessor's international aspirations. Apart from having to deal with the hefty royal debts he had inherited (for artillery, a large navy, and embassies abroad), he also had to manage the divisions between French Catholic supporters and those who wanted Scotland to adopt a more financially prudent stance of neutrality. James V's two successive French marriages indicated where his loyalties lied. His support for France and the papacy cost him valuable support from the Scottish nobility (especially the Protestants), as did his penchant for extracting wealth to finance his campaigns.

Their apathy for the king proved to be fatal when Henry VIII attacked Scotland in 1542. After his small army was routed near the border at Solway Moss in 1542, James V suffered from a fatal mental breakdown. His legitimate infant sons had perished (possibly due to nervous prostration), leaving behind one surviving female legitimate child: Mary Stuart (Mary, Queen of Scots).[83]

Born a mere week after her father's death, Mary was eventually shipped off to France for protection at age five by her mother, Mary of Guise.[84] In her absence, Mary of Guise served as acting regent after fending off Henry VIII's attempt to control his great-niece. Mary had a sheltered and privileged upbringing at the court of King Henry II and Queen Catherine de Médici, where her welfare was overseen by her mother's influential relatives. She hunted, danced, learned Latin, Italian, Spanish, and Greek, and grew to speak French as her first language. In other words, she became a Frenchwoman instead of a Scot.[85]

Mary's coming of age coincided with the tumultuous Scottish Reformation. A 1560 statistic reveals the extent to which the Scottish Catholic Church had succumbed to corruption of the financial kind: the church's annual revenue that year was estimated to be £400,000 (ten times the crown's revenue). Access to such ungodly wealth had attracted unspiritual nobles who were more interested in gaining tenure of church lands, using church property to their own ends, and collecting church revenues. As a result, Protestantism was increasingly gaining favor as a genuinely spiritual institution.

The European Reformation had been instigated by Martin Luther, a German Augustinian monk who insisted that the scriptures should be every Christian's guiding text. He rejected the Pope's authority (an action that could lead to charges of heresy and death by burning at the stake at the time) and all Church practices that were not explicitly included within the Bible. With support from several German princes and the introduction of the printing press, Luther was able to spread his theories across Christian Europe – effectively creating bitter divisions between Catholics and Protestants in many nations, including Scotland.

Mary's Catholic affiliations set her against the prevailing religious trends of her time. Her father James V had merely flirted with Protestant ideas to incentivize the Pope to grant him various tax concessions. When he died, however, Scotland's status as a staunchly Catholic nation was already in question. While traditionally Catholic, technological and social changes in Scotland had placed it increasingly at odds with Rome and its ancient doctrines. While Mary was blissfully unaware as a young child, both France and England waged a war to arrange for her hand in marriage. France was Catholic; England's Henry VIII had recently converted to Protestantism. During the "Rough Wooing", England launched several military invasions to force Mary's hand in marriage. The French retaliated by supporting the Scottish army with their own men and firepower. In the end, the French emerged the victor.

Mary's mother thus brokered her first marriage, which sealed the diplomatic relationship between Scotland and France. She married Francis II,[86] the eldest son of Henry and Catherine, in April 1558. As a child ruler, Mary's prospects were nevertheless not entirely dim. Her noteworthy beauty—red-gold hair, amber-colored eyes, and statuesque height—and regal upbringing helped her embody the ideal of a Renaissance princess and earned a fair amount of admiration and support from the Scottish people. Her lack of political cunning, however, would eventually spell her downfall.

The Scottish Renaissance monarchy that James IV and James V had consolidated under the Stewart dynasty hung on a precipice.

Protestant activism and anti-French sentiment brought about a revolt against Mary of Guise in 1559. Monasteries were plundered and England's Queen Elizabeth I[87] was prompted to send in English troops to suppress French ambitions on Scotland. After Mary of Guise's death in June the following year, France and England both agreed to withdraw their troops from Scotland via the Treaty of Edinburgh.

Mary would eventually return to Scotland as an eighteen-year-old widow after the premature death of her husband in 1560 (due to an ear infection). While she was still abroad, Scotland's official religion was reformed to Protestantism. Her return to the British Isles was certainly unwelcomed. The Scottish nobility saw her as an undesirable Roman Catholic princess, while Elizabeth I saw her status as the next in line to the English throne (via her Tudor ancestry) as a threat. Elizabeth herself had divisions between Catholics and Protestants to contend with on English soil. The English Roman Catholics considered her to be an illegitimate queen, since her father Henry VIII had divorced Catherine of Aragon to marry her mother Anne Boleyn. They conspired to dethrone Elizabeth I and replace her with Mary.

Despite this treacherous political landscape, Mary initially managed a successful reign as the Queen of Scotland. With the help of her half-brother James, earl of Moray,[88] she practiced a policy of religious tolerance and charmed the common people with her beauty and grace. She also brokered a semblance of peace with the difficult Scottish nobility, who were more interested in pursuing their own ends than demonstrating any real loyalty to the crown. Mary's decision to follow her heart instead of her head catalyzed the events that led to her tragic downfall.

In July 1565, she decided to marry her handsome cousin Henry Stewart, earl of Darnley.[89] This decision further alienated Elizabeth, who did not appreciate Mary marrying a Tudor descendant. Jealous of Darnley's ascent to power, her half-brother James rebelled and stopped supporting her. Darnley had little merit as a spouse or political ally. His capacity for petty cruelty is best demonstrated by his decision to murder Mary's Italian secretary and confidant David Rizzio[90] right in front of her. (He alleged that Rizzio was having an affair with his wife). With the help of a group of Protestant nobles, he ambushed Mary as she dined with Rizzio and five close friends. Mary was heavily pregnant with Darnley's child at the time, but this did nothing to stop them from dragging Rizzio from the table. He was stabbed no less than 56 times in the adjacent room.

The arrival of Mary's son James did nothing to halt the deterioration of their marriage. Now in possession of an heir, Mary looked for a means to exit this untenable arrangement. Her actions would prove to be highly controversial, even if the full complicity in the death of her husband remains unknown. What is known is this: during the night of February 9, 1567, Darnley was recovering from a serious illness in a house on the outer parts of Edinburgh. This house was blown up, and Darnley was found strangled to death (he survived the blast and was attempting an escape when killed). A mere three months later, Mary married the Earl of Bothwell, an adventurer and the chief suspect in Darnley's murder.[91]

Mary's opponents alleged that she had been in an adulterous relationship with Bothwell, who had murdered Darnley to rise to power. Another theory was that Darnley had been plotting to murder Mary, but was killed by his own trap. Whatever her intentions and affections for Bothwell, it was a politically suicidal move. It reflected Mary's own deteriorating mental health and lack of a wise counselor to support her decision-making process in a treacherous time. The Scottish nobility revolted against their queen and her consort. They were permanently separated at Carberry Hill on June 15, 1567. Bothwell was exiled and imprisoned until his death in 1578.

Mary was sentenced to imprisonment in Lochleven Castle and forced to abdicate. Her one-year-old son James was crowned as King of Scotland in her place. Mary still had supporters though who helped her escape from her prison in 1568. After they were defeated at Langside, she fled to England to seek refuge under the care of her cousin Elizabeth I. Instead, Elizabeth I deftly used Darnley's murder as an excuse to imprison Mary in England. As her half-brother James Moray excelled at being the regent of Scotland, Mary languished in several prisons over the following 18 years of her life.

Elizabeth I was pressured by her Protestant supporters to eliminate her Catholic rival to the throne, but she was not unsympathetic to her cousin's plight. She kept Mary under surveillance and left her to find some peace in religion, embroidery, and small pets. Mary pleaded unsuccessfully for her freedom and began turning to more risky means of securing it. She became the central figure of various Catholic plots that wanted to assassinate Elizabeth and replace her with Mary but was not directly involved in any of them. When she began corresponding with Anthony Babington who was scheming to depose Elizabeth, her death sentence was sealed.

Francis Walsingham, Elizabeth's principal secretary and "spymaster," intercepted those letters and used them as evidence to convince Elizabeth to place her cousin under trial. Her status as the sovereign queen of Scotland could not save her from being found guilty of treason. She was condemned to death in October 1586. Her cousin hesitated before signing her death warrant, but she eventually placed her name on the dotted line. As long as she lived, Mary would pose a danger to the English throne. She was executed at Fotheringhay Castle, at the age of 44, on February 8, 1587. Years of physical inactivity had robbed her of her health and beauty, but she met her end with an unnerving grace. When her son, James VI of Scotland,[92] succeeded Elizabeth I as the king of England in 1603, he exhumed her body from Peterborough Cathedral. Her final resting place was a stately monument in the vault of King Henry VII's

Chapel in Westminster Abbey. This was his royal way of commemorating the mother he never knew—the woman who allowed him to become the king of Scotland *and* England.

Mary's legacy as a compelling ill-fated figure of Scottish and English history lives on. Her opponents denounced her as an adulteress and a conniving murderess, whereas others saw her as a tragic and romantic character deserving of sympathy. Modern cinema has certainly been sympathetic to her life story. She has been portrayed (as the main protagonist) by four-time Oscar-winning American actress Katharine Hepburn in 1936, English actress Vanessa Redgrave in 1971, and bilingual French actress Camille Rutherford in 2013. Irish and American Oscar-nominated actress Saoirse Ronan will portray her as a strong-minded warrior queen in *Mary Queen of Scots*, an upcoming film that will be released on December 7, 2018, in the United States.

Chapter 10 – The King of Great Britain

Unlike his mother, James VI did not fall victim to the bitter divisions between the Scottish factions who were pro-Catholic and those who were Protestant-leaning. His early life was fairly isolated, but his solid education helped to prepare him not only for the Scottish kingship but also as a monarch on the European stage. When he was 12, he got his first taste of leading the government when the earl of Morton was removed from the regency in 1578. In 1581, he took decisive control over his kingdom from the succession of regents who had been in power ever since he was born. He would soon prove that he was no longer content with serving as a puppet for the various factions vying for supremacy and power.

He soon realized that he had more to gain from an alliance with Elizabeth I as opposed to joining forces with all her opponents. In 1586, they became formal allies via the Treaty of Berwick. When Elizabeth signed Mary of Scots' death warrant the following year, James VI merely voiced meek and formal protests. With his mother dead and Elizabeth I facing old age without an heir, he was effectively next in line to the English throne.

By the time James VI married Anne,[93] the daughter of Frederick II of Denmark, he had established a firm centralized authority. With great political intelligence and a knack for diplomacy, he played off the Protestant and Roman Catholic nobles against each other to maintain his position. He also had the effective aid of the Octavians, a group of commissioners that helped him rival Elizabeth I in terms of the absoluteness of her rule. Despite being baptized as a Catholic at Stirling Castle as a young boy, James VI became a devout

Presbyterian.[94] He arranged to appoint himself the head of Scotland's Presbyterian Church, a position which granted him the power to appoint its bishops.

In March 1603, the moment that James VI had been waiting for arrived. Elizabeth I died, allowing James VI of Scotland to become

James I of England and Ireland. This transition of power was surprisingly smooth; James VI relocated to London and only returned to Scotland once after that (in 1617). The first few years of his reign were a time of peace and prosperity for both kingdoms. After only one year on the throne, he ended England's costly war with Spain. He also tried to arrange a marriage between the Spanish Infanta (Philip III's eldest daughter Anne) and his son but was unsuccessful. His daughter Elizabeth was married to Frederick, the elector of the palatinate (a historical region in Germany) and a leader of the German Protestants.

James VI's early education inculcated literary ambitions that were quite unusual in princes and kings. This can be partly attributed to the influence of his tutor George Buchanan[95], a noted historian and poet. Over the years, his body of political writings grew to include *The True Lawe of Free Monarchies* (1598) and *Basilikon Doron* (1599), as well as a collection of poems and political essays. His most famous and enduring literary contribution, however, was the newly authorized English translation of the Bible which was published in 1611. The King James Version[96] of the Bible became the standard issue for over 250 years since it was first published. There was a need for the English Bible to be revised after the Reformation, since many deemed the existing translations to be "corrupt and not answerable to the truth of the original." The King James Version was inevitably found to be lacking in one regard or the other depending on who was doing the judging (Catholics wanted the new translation of the Bible to be more supportive of their doctrines vis-à-vis Protestantism; Puritans wanted James VI to introduce some of the Scottish Church's more radical ideas), but it is widely acknowledged as one of early modern England's most important literary accomplishments.

James VI was not content to simply have England and Scotland be symbolically united under the same monarch. He styled himself "king of Great Britain" with the aim of erasing the bitter divisions between England and Scotland, with the grandiose objective of unifying them into one entity. Weeks after he arrived in London, he proclaimed his grand ambitions for uniting the two longtime rivals. The commission of English and Scottish Members of Parliaments (MPs) that was established to assess the viability of such an endeavor ultimately found themselves being unable to agree on this venture. They did, however, agree that England should repeal all of the hostile laws that it had introduced against the Scots over the years. At this point in time, Great Britain remained more of a symbolic aspiration than an actuality. The Union Jack, which combined the crosses of St. George and St. Andrew, was nevertheless there to stay.

Naturally, there were blemishes on James VI's legacy. Apart from failing to convince Westminster of the viability of a total union between England and Scotland, he often antagonized them with his theories about a monarch's divine right to rule (i.e., royal absolutism).[97] He also incurred their wrath by constantly demanding additional funds to pay for all of his extravagant expenditures (his spending habits were especially intolerable given the costs that had recently been incurred through England's long war with Spain). In the end, no compromise could be reached between the dictatorial king and an increasingly self-assertive Parliament that demanded the right to shape public policy. In 1611, James VI dissolved the Parliament after a series of conflicts. After the death of James VI's competent chief minister Robert Cecil in 1612, his judgment only deteriorated over the years.

Despite these shortcomings, England and Scotland were closer than ever before during James VI's reign. The earlier centuries of incessant conflict were replaced by increasing cultural and economic assimilation (the two kingdoms remained politically distinct, despite James VI's desire for a complete union). The English and Scottish Churches were also united in their shared interests in preserving the Reformation and fending off Roman Catholic plans to undermine it.

A new dilemma arose in the Scottish national consciousness. Did they want to pursue a complete and totalizing union with England or revert back to a time when the two kingdoms were utterly separated?

Chapter 11 – The Union and The Scottish Enlightenment

James VI died in March 1625 and was succeeded by a son (Charles I[98]) who had no interest in realizing his father's vision of a united Scotland and England. And yet, the Act of Union[99] would be signed in less than a century after he assumed the throne. On May 1, 1707, Scotland and England united under the name of Great Britain. For the first time in history, the Scottish Parliament would be disbanded; its MPs would represent Scottish interests through their seats in Westminster.

The road to this political milestone was anything but smooth sailing. Like his father, Charles I's insistence on his divine right to rule ran afoul of an increasingly critical and antagonistic Parliament. Having been raised in England all his life, his utter lack of affinity with Scotland and its people and institutions earned him the disfavor of the Scottish nobility. He alienated them further by pursuing wars with Spain and France, which advanced English interests but disrupted Scottish trade interests. By 1641, a revolutionary situation was at hand in both kingdoms after Charles I attempted to implement anti-Catholic changes on the English and Scottish Churches. After two bitter civil wars, Charles I's supporters were defeated. He was charged with high treason and "other high crimes against the realm of England." On January 30, 1649, he was sentenced to death.

Oliver Cromwell,[100] an English soldier and statesman who had led the Parliament against Charles I, then assumed his role as the lord protector of England, Scotland, and Ireland. He declared England to be a commonwealth and free state. Determined to restore England to the status it enjoyed under Elizabeth I, he introduced a full and incorporating parliamentary union in Scotland. Despite the general lack of support, his administrative efficiency and impartial judiciary effectively maintained order and peace across both kingdoms. Any possibility of dissent was stifled by Cromwell's readiness to use sheer force.

The monarchy was eventually restored on May 14, 1660, when Charles II was proclaimed king of Great Britain and Ireland. When he was succeeded by his brother James VII,[101] however, James VII's deep desire to establish an absolutist rule in both kingdoms and to reinstate a Catholic monarchy instigated widespread turmoil.

His Protestant opponents invited Prince William of Orange,[102] husband of James' Protestant daughter Mary, to lead the charge against their intolerably pro-Catholic king. William's show of force was successful, forcing James VII to escape to France. Prince William III of Orange was offered the English crown in April 1689 and the Scottish crown the following month. The 1689 Bill of Rights nevertheless stipulated that monarchs could no longer govern without the consent of their parliaments.

These prolonged periods of internal conflict had severely weakened the Scottish economy. When the idea of a union between England and Scotland resurfaced as William of Orange was offered the English crown, the Scottish elite were in favor of the proposal. The union would also help to enshrine Protestantism in both kingdoms and stave off attacks from ex-King James and his pro-Catholic supporters. There was nevertheless still a significant amount of anti-English sentiment among the Scottish masses. It would take far more extenuating circumstances—William III's unexpected death from a horse-riding fall, a new war between Britain and France, a Scottish Parliament revolt, and additional accommodations for Scotland in terms of trade, religion, and taxes—for Scotland to finally warm up to the idea of a union. They were partly persuaded by an attractive carrot (access to a unified free trade area) and two dire sticks (England would ban all imports of Scottish staple products if Scotland refused the terms for a union, and Scots would lose their rights to English property).[103]

The benefits of the Union to Scotland with its guarantee of free trade and safeguards for Scotland's national church and legal system can be seen in the Scottish Enlightenment.[104] One may not simply conclude a clear cause and effect scenario here, but it is evident that the newfound era of peace and prosperity under this arrangement allowed for the unprecedented evolution of Scottish intellectual life. Scottish intellectual accomplishments from the 1750s onward earned Edinburgh descriptors as a "hotbed of genius."

From the sciences to philosophy to economics, Scottish thinkers became international leaders in their field. The Scottish Enlightenment's hall of fame includes historian and philosopher David Hume[105], philosopher Adam Smith[106], historian William Robertson, poet Robert Burns, architect Robert Adam and his brother James, mathematician Colin Maclaurin, physiologist William Cullen, chemist Joseph Black, geologist James Hutton[107], and engineers James Watt and Thomas Telford. Their wide-ranging intellectual accomplishments were evidence of a robust Scottish educational system, which advocated for wide-ranging intellectual curiosity and the practical applications of knowledge.

James Hutton, David Hume and Adam Smith would eventually be recognized as three of the most influential intellectuals in the history of Europe. Hutton's contributions as a geologist were crucial in ushering in an age of religious skepticism. Hutton introduced the then-groundbreaking concept of uniformitarianism, which explains the various features of the Earth's crust by means of natural processes over geologic time such as erosion, sedimentation, deposition, and upthrusting. By using precise calculations to determine the age of rocks in Scotland, Hutton had scientific evidence that the earth was much, much older than the 6,000 years the Bible had claimed. Hutton's findings contributed to his conviction that it was scientific discoveries, and not religion, that should be used to understand the laws of the natural world. His 1785 publication *A Theory of the Earth* became the founding text for modern geology.

On the other hand, David Hume made immense contributions to the field of philosophy. An intellectual of many stripes – philosopher, historian, economist, essayist – he was especially known for his skepticism and philosophical empiricism. At only 28, he returned to Scotland from France with the publication of his groundbreaking work *A Treatise on Human Nature.* Like Hutton, Hume was invested in a secular and scientific worldview that moved firmly away from the Christian theological worldview that had shaped much of Scotland's past. He drew from the works of English physicist Sir Isaac Newton and English philosopher John Locke. He intended to explain humanity without referring to God or religion and turned to scientific reasoning to do so. For Hume, morality was not a product of God's creation. Instead, it was a product of human reason and sentiment – a practical imperative that motivates us to differentiate between right and wrong. Hume understood that we are not purely rational beings; our emotions, sentiments, and passions played a significant role in shaping our thoughts and rationality. Hume was also a brave and outspoken critic of religion; he boldly questioned the veracity of miracles. On his deathbed, Hume was cheerfully unperturbed by the possibility of a Christian afterlife where he would be judged harshly for his atheism.

Finally, Adam Smith was a moral philosopher that is credited as the father of modern economics. *An Inquiry into the Nature and Causes of the Wealth of Nations* is a seminal text that is still widely read in economics courses across the world. Smith was strongly motivated to understand how money was circulated and its impact on society. Smith's scholarship was crucial in understanding how the rapidly evolving commercial economy that emerged throughout the Industrial Revolution had bearings on everyday life and national policy. Smith was invested in economic efficiency and free trade, but he was not oblivious to the detrimental effects that the pursuit of wealth could engender. He deemed economic progress to be synonymous with societal progress. The purely profit-driven interests of Glasgow's tobacco lords and the existence of slavery were deemed to be undesirable rungs on the ladder towards a more enlightened civilization. Smith's economic ideas were also crucial to Britain's decision to end the American War of Independence. Smith's position as an eminent economic thinker allowed him to influence the British Prime Minister that Britain would gain more wealth by trading with American instead of attempting to ensure that it remained a subservient colony.

Chapter 12 – The Industrial Revolution

In the early 1700s, Scotland was mostly a rural and agricultural economy. It only had a population of one million people, with a relatively small portion based in its modest urban townships. Within the course of a single lifetime, everything changed. By the 1820s, the effects of the Industrial Revolution[108] were unmistakable. The scientific theories that had been conceptualized during the Scottish Enlightenment swiftly turned into practical applications that could be turned into hearty profits in a capitalist world.

Scotland's population rose dramatically. People left the countryside and traditional farm life for manufacturing towns, which eventually became bustling cities. There were approximately 1.5 million people in Scotland during the start of the 19th century. By the end of the 20th century, this number had tripled to over 4.5 million people. A significant portion of this rise can be attributed to immigrants, particularly Irish immigrants who were fleeing the prospect of starvation during the Irish Potato Famine (1845–1849).[109]

This population rise was also partly the byproduct of crucial advancements in medicine, healthcare, and public health standards. These improvements reduced the mortality rate in the face of previously fatal epidemic diseases. Meanwhile, the scientific innovations that were assimilated into traditional agricultural practices allowed fewer farmers to produce enough produce to feed a larger population. Southeastern farmers were praised for their efficiency, northeastern farmers for their cattle and beef, and Ayrshire (a county in the south-west) for the large quantities of quality milk their cows produced.[110]

Innovations in chemistry (e.g. the use of chlorine to bleach linen) helped make the Scottish textile industry surpass agriculture. Linen production became more efficient than ever before with the use of newly discovered chemicals and the adoption of English inventions like Hargreave's spinning jenny, Arkwright's water frame, and Crompton's mule. These inventions transformed the weaving process, radically increasing output, productivity, and competitiveness. Instead of relying on human power alone, these new spinning machines were powered by massive water wheels. The old tradition of men working on handlooms were replaced by an efficient factory system. Women and children were roped into the workforce, spending long hours toiling for relatively low wages.

During the 1830s, heavy industry replaced textiles as the most important component of the Scottish economy. The production of coal and iron rose tremendously, facilitating the popularization of railways, steam locomotives, and ships. The use of canals and horses as the dominant form of transportation slowly became obsolete. If the first phase of the Industrial Revolution mainly consisted of old industries becoming more efficient through the adoption of new technologies, the second phase was driven by Scottish innovations themselves. Henry Bell (1767-1830) built the *Comet*, the first successful passenger steamship, in 1812. It catalyzed the birth of the Scottish shipbuilding industry and the railway industry. James Watt (1736–1819) did not invent the steam engine as commonly believed (it had existed since the early 18th century), but he did invent the separate condenser (which reduced the amount of water steam engines needed while allowing them to produce more power).

The introduction of an extensive railway network helped Scotland to make significant economic progress during the Victorian era. When Queen Victoria assumed the throne in 1827, there were only a few Scottish railway lines in existence. These were mainly used to transport coal and other industrial raw materials between the bustling urban hubs of Glasgow, Edinburgh, and Dundee. In 1843, the Edinburgh-Glasgow railway line opened, catalyzing a national obsession with railways. Within a single generation, practically all of Scotland's railways were built – constituting some of the world's most ambitious engineering projects at the time. Railway tracks were built between small villages and major towns, stretching across all directions. Thanks to the advent of efficient steam engines, journeys that would have taken days on horse-drawn carriages were now completed in a matter of hours.

There was, of course, a dark side to all this intellectual, economic and technological progress. The extensive railway network effectively bridged the distance between the urban centers and the countryside, allowing tourism in rural Scotland to boom. Urban growth during the Victorian era had created dirty, overcrowded and polluted cities, with Glasgow being the primary example. The lack of adequate housing for the huge influx of migrants had led to the sprawl of slums with dire standards of living. With over 20,000 people forced to lived in shabby housing and practically no sanitation, one can only imagine the effect of such conditions on the body and mind:

> "In the very centre of the city there was an accumulated mass of squalid wretchedness unequalled in any other town in the British Dominions. There was concentrated everything wretched, dissolute, loathsome and pestilential. Dunghills lie in the vicinity of dwellings, and from the extremely defective sewerage filth of every kind constantly accumulates."[111]

These dismal living conditions were incredibly conducive to disease. Glasgow soon became a hotbed for typhus and typhoid. Scotland's participation in the global British Empire also led to a deadly outbreak of cholera. In 1832, the first cholera outbreak in Scotland killed three thousand people in Glasgow alone. All the public health advances that had been achieved since the Black Plague were temporarily reversed as death rates soared to 17th-century heights. It appears obvious now, but the link between dirt and disease was not immediately apparent then. It was only after the subsequent cholera epidemics of 1848 and 1853 that the medical community identified the filthy living conditions as a problem that had to be solved. The introduction of an expensive sewage system and a clean water supply from Loch Katrine from 1850 and 1875 was crucial in improving sanitation and public health standards in Glasgow.

Eager to escape the grimness of city life, many wealthier Scots took the opportunity to breathe in the fresh air and enjoy the stunning vistas of the Scottish countryside.[112] They also developed appetites for hunting deer, shooting birds, and fishing. By the 1890s, there were widespread concerns that urban-rural tourism was devastating the countryside and causing various species of bird and deer to tether towards extinction.

Apart from the rising pollution levels and the desecration of nature for the extraction of raw materials, Scotland's relentless appetite for wealth and progress incurred heavy ethical costs. As Scotland looked beyond its traditional trading relationships with France and the Low Countries (Netherlands, Belgium and western Germany), it became complicit in the imperial exploitation of countries and populations outside of Europe. The Scottish textile industry developed a dependence on imported cotton from India, England's prized colonial possession, as well as the slave plantations of America.

Scottish capitalists also proved to be adept at extracting profits from the Atlantic trade of tobacco. There were no tobacco plantations in Scotland, but Glasgow's infamous tobacco lords were able to gain a firm grip on the trade through their strategic position (Glasgow was closer to the transatlantic shipping routes than London or Bristol) and savvy use of capital. Their agents sailed out to North Carolina and Virginia to trade with the owners of small tobacco plantations. They provided credit and loaned them tools wrought from Scottish iron and Scottish-made linen (which would be repaid with takings from their future crops). As these plantations grew in size and scale with the help of their funding, so did the amount of tobacco that made its way to Glasgow's warehouses. No ship that sailed into Glasgow needed to wait very long to be fully loaded with tobacco.

Tobacco was only one component of Scotland's Three Way Trade with the rapidly evolving American economy.[113] Ships from Scotland would sail to Africa to be filled with slaves. These slaves would then be taken to either tobacco plantations in America or sugar plantations in the West Indies. The ships would return to Scottish ports with the products of this exploitative labor system (primarily sugar and tobacco). This arrangement also brought in large amounts of profits into Scotland, which could then be reinvested into the Scottish Industrial Revolution. In 1747, the Tobacco Lords became even wealthier when the French government gave Glasgow a lucrative monopoly over the supply of tobacco to France. The huge influx of money into Scotland's rising number of banks facilitated the growth of a financial industry and newfangled forms of credit.

Chapter 13 – Decline

After the triumphs of the Scottish Enlightenment and the Industrial Revolution, Scotland found itself in an arc of decline. World War I (July 8, 1914–November 11, 1918)[114] coincided not only with the loss of many Scottish lives (over 140,000 Scottish soldiers were killed), but also with widespread economic decline. Trouble was brewing even before the war. The Singer Sewing Factory strike in 1911 was a clear indication of the untenable working conditions in the majority of Scotland's factories. In 1915, the lack of housing, high rental fees, and the poor quality of existing housing led to mass rent strikes in Glasgow.

Given these generally dismal conditions, it is not surprising that many Scottish men volunteered to fight against Germany during World War I. While their Victorian English counterparts thought little of the prospect of being a soldier, their Scottish counterparts' psyche had been indelibly shaped by years of tribal infighting and conflict with the English military. In 1914, Scotland made up less than 10 percent of Britain's pre-War population. However, Scotsmen comprised of 13 percent of the volunteers that enlisted in the British Army between 1914 and 1915. To distinguish themselves from their English comrades, they fought in plaid kilts, wore sporrans (a traditional Scottish pouch that functioned as a pocket on the pocket-free kilt), and marched to the military tunes emitted by bagpipes. On the home front, Scotland suffered from its first air raid during this time. On 2 April 1916, two German Zeppelins dropped bombs over the fields of Northumberland and the city of Edinburgh. Between 100, 000 and 148, 000 Scottish men and women died during World War I.

The marriage and birth rates increased after World War I ended in 1918, leading to Scotland's own "baby boom" in 1920. That year, 137,000 babies were born – a dramatic statistic that was not matched by the baby boom Scotland experienced after World War II.

By 1919, Scotland's population was estimated to reach 4.8 million people – the highest number of people since 1855. Scotland's population would eventually peak at nearly 4.9 million in 1922 when the post-war optimism waned in the face of economic hardship.

The socialist movement and trade union activism only intensified as it became evident that the incredible expansion of heavy industry in the 1920s was actually an overexpansion. The war had created a short-lived demand for production from Scotland's coal mining, shipbuilding and engineering industries. After it ended, the fall in demand for new ships decimated Scottish shipbuilding by a staggering 90% of its initial size. Meanwhile, increasing foreign competition put over 50% of Scotland's iron furnaces out of business by 1927. Scottish industry also suffered as Germany, Eastern Europe and Russia ceased to be export markets for Scottish goods due to political factors. The introduction of new technologies and production methods also played a role in reducing the number of jobs that required manual labor.

The economic depression that plagued Britain from the 1920s onward was particularly acute in Scotland. Scotland was home to the poorest living conditions in all of Britain and high rates of unemployment. With the economy in ruins after four years of warfare, thousands of Scots decide to leave the British Isles for the chance of a better life in the colonies. Between 1841–1931, over two million Scots emigrated abroad – the highest emigration rate for any European country during this period. Unskilled laborers sought better fortunes on the shores of Canada and Australia, while their skilled counterparts sought to recreate their middle-class lives in South Africa and the United States. This "brain drain" cost Scotland many of its skilled and educated men and women. Meanwhile, approximately 749,000 Scots relocated to other parts of Great Britain (primarily England).

It is not surprising that these trying economic conditions were a breeding ground of political radicalism. When the General Strike unfolded in 1926 (where all union workers across the nation refused to work unless they were granted better pay and improved working conditions), tanks and soldiers lined the streets in anticipation of a Communist revolution. The Liberal Party found their influence waning, while the Unionists, Labour, and the Scottish National Party (SNP) gained widespread support and popularity.

Scottish resilience was tested once again during World War II (September 1, 1939–September 2, 1945)[115], when Scotland became a target for aggressive German bombing raids. This time, Scottish civilians would not be spared the suffering that their sailors, pilots, and soldiers endured as they fought against Adolf Hitler's formidable army. Nazi pilots took aim at Scotland's hubs to target its crucial heavy industry factories. During the nights of March 13 and 14, 1941, the industrial hub of Clydebank in Glasgow suffered from sustained bombing.

The death count on the home front was reduced by the pre-emptive evacuation of children and their mothers in the cities to the countryside, but this also caused a major disruption to everyday life.

[116] Many families had to be separated during the evacuation process, causing significant psychological trauma to the younger children. They also had to make do with strict food rationing during the war, which limited their daily food intake to small portions of tea, jam, butter, sugar, and cheese.

After the first wave of bombing raids, the Scots lived in fear of subsequent attacks. They were thankfully spared the agony and devastation when Hitler decided to focus German military efforts on an ill-advised attack on Russia. When the Axis parties finally surrendered, Scotland had lost approximately 34,000 soldiers and 6,000 civilians. Efforts were made to reduce unemployment and restore the health of the Scottish economy, but to mixed results. Agricultural productivity was sustained, but Scotland's heavy industries (e.g., shipbuilding and coal mining) would never recover.

Chapter 14: Scottish Feminism

Scotland's involvement in the two world wars had major and longstanding ramifications on gender roles in Scottish society. Before the war, Scottish women had been pressured to conform to the Victorian ideal of being the "angel in the home". Women from the middle and working classes were very much expected to faithfully perform the duties of a wife and mother. The opportunity to attend university or to pursue a career alongside their male counterparts was typically out of the equation. The men were expected to bring home the proverbial bacon, while the women were expected to take care of the home and children.[117]

This did not mean that women were completely absent from the workforce prior to the war. Young unmarried women, spinsters, and widows who did not have a man to rely on often pursued careers in stereotypically "feminine" professions: nursing, childcare, and teaching. They were paid less than their male counterparts and not considered to be of equal standing, but these forms of employment nevertheless allowed them to take up roles and positions beyond the confines of domesticity.

Working class women – who often had larger families than their middle-class counterparts – were usually forced to work due to economic necessity. To supplement their husband's income, they often worked on a part-time basis as a cook, cleaner, or nanny for wealthier families. The labor they performed – in addition to the challenging duties of caring for their own children – were nevertheless rarely considered as "real work" – which was then perceived to be an exclusively male domain. When a 1911 census revealed that only 1 in 20 working Scottish women were married, it most probably excluded all the part-time work performed by working-class women.

The First World War radically altered this status quo. As large numbers of able-bodied Scottish men enlisted in the military, they left behind sizable numbers of vacancies in the factories. Scottish women thus seized the opportunity to perform work roles that they had previously been excluded from. They also gained a political voice by joining Trade Unions. When the men who survived the war returned home and resumed their factory work, they found that their female counterparts were in a significantly stronger bargaining position.[118]

The opportunity to participate in the workforce had been particularly advantageous for working-class women, who had been largely overlooked by the pre-war suffragette movement. Before WWI, the Women's Social and Political Union (WSPU) had largely advocated for voting rights to be extended to middle-class, property-owning women. This previously exclusive and narrow advocacy was democratized when large numbers of working-class women gained a platform for their concerns via trade union membership. In 1918, women over 30 could vote regardless of class. In 1928, women finally gained equal voting rights.[119]

Societal changes in attitudes towards sex, contraception, marriage and motherhood during the early 20th century also played a significant part in the lives of Scottish women. The very same year that women over 30 gained the opportunity to vote, Edinburgh-born Marie Stopes[120] published an important treatise of marriage and feminism titled *Married Love.* Stopes decried the traditional gendered division of labor which prevent women from fully participating in public life. She advocated for a more equal division of household labor and childcaring duties that would allow women to pursue their own careers and lives beyond the domestic sphere. She was also a pioneer in her advocacy for birth control, which granted women more control over their bodies and life choices. Contraception may be taken for granted today, but this was a highly controversial topic during Stopes' lifetime. She went against the Pope and church leaders, but she did have the backing of the medical community. Stopes was not content with being a bestselling author and public figure. She went on to form the Mother's Clinic for Constructive Birth Control in Holloway, London, in 1921. She also influenced the formation of the National Birth Control Association in 1931, which paved the way for the introduction of The Family Planning Act in 1967. Stopes' influence is evident in the consistent decline in Scottish birth rates, which halved between the late 1870s and early 1930s.

The Second World War allowed Scottish women to participate more actively in the labor market once again. As their male counterparts took to the skies, seas, and battlefields, they staffed the Women's Land Army and vacant factories. While they were barred from battling on the frontlines, they also supported the British military through their participation in the Women's Voluntary Service (WVS), Auxiliary Territorial Service (ATS), and the Women's Auxiliary Air Force (WAAF). The changing attitudes towards women's capabilities and the urgency of the war allowed Scottish women to take on highly technical engineering jobs. For example, over 10, 000 women were employed at the Rolls-Royce factory at Hillington (near Glasgow), where they built the Merlin engines that were essential to Spitfires and Lancaster Bombers.

Scottish women still struggled to gain equal pay. A larger proportion of women nevertheless managed to remain the workforce after World War II ended (when compared to World War I). This was partly due to the recovering economy and the creation of the Welfare State. The availability of state benefits was particularly beneficial to the working classes. With more career opportunities and government aid (housing, healthcare, and childcare) for their children and elderly dependents, they were able to make great strides in improving their overall standard of living. By the 1960s, most Scottish women who worked were married – there was effectively no longer a stigma against working mothers and wives. The decline of the heavy industries in the 1970s led to more job opportunities in clerical work, secretarial work, the service sector, and light manufacturing – precisely the kind of jobs that were less inclined to discriminate against women. Full parity remains a distant reality, but there is no denying the great strides that Scottish women have achieved in education, the labor force, and field of political representation.

While Mary of Scots had once been perceived as an unfit ruler due to her gender, Nicola Sturgeon[121] made history as Scotland's first woman leader in 2014. Born in 1970, Sturgeon cited British Prime Minister Margaret Thatcher as her inspiration for participating in politics for a young age. At only 16, Sturgeon decided to join the Scottish National Party. Thatcher, who was known around the world as the "Iron Lady", as a positive role model in that demonstrating that a woman could reach the uppermost ranks of political power. As a policymaker, however, Sturgeon found little common ground with her. As a teenager, Sturgeon was deeply opposed to Thatcher's conservative policies – which were highly unpopular in Scotland.

Sturgeon went on to pursue a law degree at the University of Glasgow and became a solicitor for a Glasgow law firm. Her ambitions nevertheless remained within the field of politics. During Britain's 1992 general election, Sturgeon became Scotland's youngest parliamentary candidate (she was nearly 22). She did not win a seat, but her place at the table was earned in 1999. As a member of the Scottish Parliament, she took on a prominent role in the National Executive Committee. She worked in the domains of health, education and justice.

In June 2004, Sturgeon made her ambitions for the leadership of her SNP known when John Swinney resigned. She eventually withdrew her candidacy in favor of Alex Salmond, who had been the party leader before Swinney replaced him in 2000. Sturgeon became Salmond's running mate and was rewarded with the deputy leader position when he won the election. Since Salmond was an MP at Westminster and not a member of the Scottish Parliament in

Edinburgh, however, Sturgeon was the de facto leader of the SNP contingent in Edinburgh. She gained a solid reputation for her leadership and oratory prowess. Under her leadership, SNP emerged as the largest party in the Scottish Parliament after the 2007 elections. Salmon became Scotland's first minister, while Sturgeon became his deputy and minister for public health and well-being. In 2014, Salmond resigned as Scotland's first minister and leader of the SNP – allowing Sturgeon to take her place as Scotland's first female head of state since Mary of Scots.

Chapter 15: LGBT Rights in Scotland

As with women's rights, Scotland has made significant progress in the field of LGBT rights in recent decades. For much of its history, religious attitudes led to widespread discrimination against gay, lesbian, bisexual and transgender individuals in Scotland. Scottish attitudes towards the question of homosexuality did not significantly depart from the United Kingdom until after World War II.[122]

In post-war Britain, there was a significant increase in the prosecution of gay men for homosexual crimes in England and Wales. Policemen would often use a strategy of entrapment – posturing as gay men looking for sexual encounters in popular "cruising" spots – to arrest men who were actively seeking for sexual liaisons. Some of the most high-profile arrests in British history include the English author Oscar Wilde (in 1895), English computer scientist Alan Turing (1952), and the Wildeblood scandal (1954). The increasing frequency of arrests prompted the government to form the Wolfenden Committee in 1954. Led by Sir John Wolfenden, it consulted legal representatives, religious leaders, legislators, and civic leaders to address the issue of homosexual behavior.

In 1957, the Departmental Committee on Homosexual Offences and Prostitution in Great Britain submitted its report.[123] This marked the first time that a British government participated in public discourse on homosexuality and the rights of sexual minorities in the nation. While the report did not condone or sanction homosexual behavior or same-sex relationships, it did argue that the criminalization of homosexuality was an injustice to civil liberty. It argued that one's sexual orientation and preferences was a private matter of morality. It also advocated for medical treatment to "correct" homosexual desires and behaviors and for children and adults to be protected from homosexual activity. The medical treatments that arrested gay men were often subjected to would be deemed highly unethical by modern standards. They usually involved electroconvulsive therapy (ECT) and estrogen therapy.

A decade later, the recommendations made by the Wolfenden Report contributed to the 1967 Sexual Offences Act. Its primary contribution to LGBT rights was the decriminalization of homosexuality in the law of England and Wales. However, Scotland and Northern Ireland were exempted from these reforms. The resistance towards the Wolfenden recommendations was particularly strong in Scotland. Dr. Gayle Davis, a social historian working at the University of Edinburgh noted that the general consensus was that Scotland was not ready to accept LGBT individuals:

> "There's a lot of resistance to Wolfenden in Scotland, there's really a great deal. Law in fact can be quite resistant - lawyers themselves. And one of the reasons, kind of ironically, is because they argue Scotland has, basically, a more lenient legal system anyway. It's actually much more difficult to be prosecuted for homosexuality in Scotland than it is in England and Wales and therefore let's not touch it. we don't need to interfere."[124]

Scottish attitudes towards homosexuality became more progressive in the 1970s and 1980s, as the sexual revolution sparked in the United States coincided with a general decline in religious beliefs. Scotland finally decriminalized homosexuality in 1980, after activist groups like the Scottish Minorities Group brought their case to the European Court of Human Rights. When the Criminal Justice (Scotland) Act was introduced, Scotland was finally on par with England and Wales in terms of LGBT rights.

Since then, Scotland has remarkably established a reputation as one of Europe's most progressive countries in the domain of LGBTI equality. The Scottish government has viewed its previous legal position on homosexuality as discrimination and made efforts to remove criminal records for gay men who were once persecuted by the justice system for their sexual orientation.[125] The 2007 Adoption and Children (Scotland) Act 2007 gave same-sex couples the opportunity to adopt children together. Another milestone was achieved with the Sexual Offences (Scotland) Act of 2009, which removed sexual orientation and gender identity from the list of legal sexual offenses.

In 2010, the Equality Act was introduced to protect LGBTI individuals from hate crimes and discrimination on the basis of their sexual orientation. It also provided legal protection for transgender individuals at all stages of the gender reassignment process. In 2014, Scotland became the first country within the United Kingdom to legalize same-sex marriage via the Marriage and Civil Partnership (Scotland) Act 2014 – which was passed by an overwhelming majority in the Scottish parliament. It also began including intersex individuals within its equality framework that year – one of the most inclusive legislation in the world. The Scottish government has also announced its partnership with the Scottish Transgender Alliance (STA), with the aim of improving public understanding of the nuances and complexities of gender identity and reassignment surgeries. It has supported LGBTI activist organizations and made efforts to alleviate the bullying of LGBTI students and youths.

Given these milestones, it is not entirely surprising that Scotland was ranked the most inclusive European nation for LGBTI equality and human rights legislation in 2015 by the European Region of the International Lesbian, Gay, Bisexual, Trans and Intersex Association (ILGA Europe).[126] Scotland met 92% of ILGA's 48-point criteria, beating other notably progressive European nations such as Belgium, Malta, and Sweden. Scotland's progressive attitudes are also evident in the fact that many of its politicians are openly gay, lesbian and bisexual. This includes Kezia Dugdale (a former leader of the Scottish Labour Party), Ruth Davidson (Leader of the Scottish Conservative Party), Patrick Harvie (co-convener of the Scottish

Green Party), and David Coburn (leader of the Scottish UK Independence Party).[127]

There have naturally been setbacks to the increasing representation of LGBTI identities in Scottish public life. In 2000, Scotland was embroiled in a bitter debate over a legal clause that banned the positive portrayal of same-sex relationships in school. While this legal clause was eventually overturned by the Scottish parliament, it led to a widespread moral panic that Scottish children would fall victim to "gay propaganda" and "gay sex lessons" in schools. The influential "Keep the Clause" campaign was a bitter reminder of the persistence of a double standard for heterosexual and homosexual relationships.

In 2017, Scotland lost its top spot on the ILGA-Europe rankings, coming in second to Malta if it was considered as a separate nation.
[128] The United Kingdom as a whole came in third, losing out slightly to Norway. The Scottish National Party (SNP) attributed this setback to the Conservatives, who were deemed to have fallen behind in making the reforms required by the equality law. Angela Crawley, the SNP candidate for Lanark and Hamilton East noted that same-sex couples were still not granted equal pension rights, and that not all LGBTI individuals were fully protected from discrimination. Further progress can also be made in providing more protection to trans and intersex individuals, as well as in providing asylum to individuals fleeing persecution for their sexual identities. As of August 2018, conversion therapy has not been banned in Scotland.

Chapter 16: The Loch Ness Monster

Despite the contributions of many Scottish intellectuals to science and modernity, the perception of Scotland as a terrain steeped in folklore, legends, myths, and superstitions persists. The stone circles of Stonehenge The unique phenomenon of Nessie, a. k. a. the Loch Ness monster, is emblematic of the longstanding Scottish appetite for legends and folklore.

The Loch Ness monster became an international sensation when the image known as the "surgeon's photograph" was widely circulated in 1934.[129] The photographic "evidence" was new, but stories and reports of the lake being home to a monster are ancient. Loch Ness comes second to Loch Lomond in terms of surface area, but it comes in first when it comes to volume (it contains more fresh water than all the lakes in Wales and England combined). It also comes in second – to Loch Morar - in terms of depth. Given these unfathomable depths, there have long been speculations as to what mysterious life forms might thrive in its impenetrable waters.

The Pict have left behind stone carvings which represent an unusual beast with flippers. A biography of St. Columba dating back to 565 A.D. is the first written account of a monster in the waters. It describes an incident where a monster bit a swimmer and then set its aggressive sights on another man. Columba made an effective intervention, ordering the monster to "go back" to the depths it came from. There have been various other sightings of a creature in the lake throughout the centuries since then.

These folktales took on a new life in the 1930s when a new road adjacent to Loch Ness allowed drivers a majestic view of the lake. In April 1933, a couple reported that they saw a large animal – akin to a "dragon or prehistoric monster" – crossing the road in front of their car and disappearing into the lake. A Scottish newspaper (the *Inverness Courier*) sensationalized the incident, which then sparked other sightings. The *Daily Mail* fueled the fires of speculation by commissioning a hunter named Marmaduke Wetherell to find the mysterious monster. He uncovered large footprints along the lake's shores, which he argued was indicative of the presence of a large animal that was 6 meters long. Zoologists from the Natural History Museum eventually pointed out that the tracks were bogus. They were all identical – impressions made with a hippopotamus leg. It is unclear if Wetherell had made the tracks himself, or if he had simply stumbled upon someone else's hoax.

The *Daily Mail* went on to print the now-iconic photograph of the Loch Ness Monster in 1934. Taken by Robert Kenneth Wilson, an English physician, it appeared to show the monster's small head and long neck from a distance. The photograph created an international interest in Nessie. Many believed that it was a plesiosaur: a long-necked marine reptile that lived during the time of the dinosaurs. The theory was that a lone plesiosaur – or a few of them – had survived the widespread extinction that marked the end of the Cretaceous phase approximately 66 million years ago. Plesiosaurs were some of the first few fossil reptiles to be discovered by paleontologists. The first plesiosaurian genus was named in 1821.

Popular culture had held fast to the idea of Nessie being a plesiosaur – a myth that is certainly more compelling than other interpretations of it being a long-necked newt, a large invertebrate, a misidentified tree-trunk, a mirage, a Greenland shark, or a large eel. Scientists have discredited the idea by pointing out that plesiosaurs were most probably cold-blooded reptiles that could only thrive in warm tropical waters – and not in the cold depths of Loch Ness.[130] They have also argued that the lake does not contain enough food to support a carnivorous reptile the size of a plesiosaur. There is also the geological fact that the loch is only 10,000 years old. Before the last ice age, it had been a frozen block of ice for nearly 20,000 years.

And yet, the myth of Nessie persists despite the lack of scientific evidence. Nessie can be found in many poems, short stories, novels, movies, and documentaries. After many monster hunters failed to find any conclusive evidence of Nessie's existence, more organized efforts were initiated. The most famous effort to find Nessie would be Operation Deepscan in 1987. This sonar exploration cost a staggering £1m. It involved a week-long trawling of the entire length of Loch Ness by a flotilla of 24 sonar-equipped boats. No large prehistoric creature was identified from this comprehensive search. Meanwhile, other photographs that seemingly depicted Nessie were proved to be hoaxes. In 1994, Wilson's enduring photograph was discredited as a plastic-and-wooden head appended to a toy submarine. The culprit was none other than Marmaduke Wetherell.

The Scottish Natural Heritage (SNH) even has a "partly serious, partly fun" code for what to do if Nessie is found.[131] Nessie would be treated as a protected new species and should not be harmed. After a DNA sample is obtained, it should be released back into Loch Ness. This plan would be updated accordingly if Nessie was found in the near future; the local businesses and communities living near Loch Ness would also have to be consulted to prepare for the inevitable arrival of tourists from all over the world. As it is, the mere myth of Nessie is enough to compel the arrival of 400,000 visitors to Loch Ness each year – which only leads to a measly ten reports of a mysterious lake-dweller each year. One can only imagine the pandemonium that might ensue if a rare species was proven to exist there.

Even if Nessie is never found, it lives on in the Scottish popular imagination. It certainly is not the only fictional animal that lives on in Scottish psyche.[132] There is a country, after all, that led to the unicorn being featured on the United Kingdom national crest. There are also kelpies, which are water spirits that resemble horses. They are often disguised as humans in Scottish folklore. The Highlanders also have various superstitions that involve fairies, which are believed to inhabit the Isle of Skye. The collective stories and myths surrounding these creatures undoubtedly contribute to Scotland's tourism industry as it enchants visitors from far and wide to seek a glimpse – or merely a sense – of Scottish magic. Nessie alone is estimated to have contributed nearly $80 million to Scotland's economy each year in the early 21st century.

Chapter 17: Postwar Scotland

The end of World War II gave way to a new world order – one where the sun had clearly set on the once all-powerful British Empire. As former British colonies across the world began demanding and securing their independence, the very idea of "Britishness" was called into question. Like their English counterparts, Scotland turned inward to examine its own place in the world as efforts to rebuild the country were underway. The Socialist government in the United Kingdom ushered in an age of austerity while the Welfare State began ingraining itself as a defining feature of British life.

In 1961, the Scottish Council for Development and Industry confessed that "if there is a panacea for Scotland's economic problems we have not found it."[133] The economy may have improved after the end of World War II, but the decline in Scottish heavy industries had still led to an unemployment rate that was twice as high as Britain's. The emerging light engineering and consumer goods industries did not create enough jobs to offset the jobs lost by the rapid disappearance of Scotland's coal-mining, steel, and shipbuilding industries. While many saw the importance of diversifying the economy, the managers of small Scottish firms and the government were relatively inefficient at taking the necessary steps to achieve this aim.

Margaret Thatcher's election as prime minister in 1979 and the policies of deregulation and privatization that followed inspired widespread sentiments that Scottish interests were being unfairly discriminated against.[134] Thatcher's stoic insistence that heavy industry be stripped of state support and allowed to perish may have been economically sound, but it led to a intense protests and anger. The Scottish miners took great pride in their line of work and never forgave Thatcher for allowing the mining industry to collapse. Scottish anti-Thatcherism sentiments culminated in the 1984 Miners' Strike, where mass protests led to violent confrontations between the Scottish miners and the police force. In 1989, another wave of protests occurred in response to the Poll Tax, which levied the same taxes on British citizens regardless of their income level. When prominent members of Thatcher's own party joined in the revolt, her political career came to an end. Thatcher's heavy-handed political style also helped to convince Scotland of the importance of having more control over its economic and political fate.

The average Scottish citizen may have been generally discontented with Westminster's decision-making, but British Prime Minister Edward Heath's decision to apply for European Economic Community (EEC) membership in the 1970s had generally positive economic effects on Scotland. The EEC was the precursor of the European Union; it had been established on 9 May 1950 to promote transnational cooperation in the light of the disastrous losses incurred during World War II. Its aim was to promote peace, cooperation and economic prosperity – in opposition to the climate of hostility and division engendered by the Cold War. Its six founding countries included Belgium, France, Germany, Italy, Luxembourg and the Netherlands. The founding countries were not merely bound by lofty ideals; they also signed a treaty to operate their heavy industries (mainly coal and steel) under common management.[135] This would prevent any member nation from channeling its resources into war efforts against its allies. In 1957, the Treaty of Rome established the European common market – a then-radical economic agreement that allowed for people, goods and services to move across borders without red tape and regulation.[136]

In 1973, the United Kingdom joined the European Union alongside Denmark and Ireland. Scotland was a major beneficiary of the EU regional policy, which aimed to alleviate economic hardship in poorer areas by allocating large amounts of money to improve infrastructure and create job opportunities.[137] Throughout the 70s, Scotland received over twice the national average per capita via EU loans and grants. Funds from the Coal and Steel Community, the European Social Fund, the European Investment Bank and the European Regional Development Fund (ERDF) helped support local businesses, as well as allowing Scotland to diversify its economy. Since it could no longer rely on its heavy industries, Scotland was encouraged to develop its financial services sector, tourism industry, cultural products, and biotechnology sector.

Despite the inflow of foreign investment from the EU, the perception that Scotland was being economically short-changed by Westminster persisted. Many politicians and members of the public believed that the United Kingdom's policies were not tailored specifically to Scotland's unique challenges, leaving it at a disadvantage to London and south-east England. The growth in national self-confidence and the belief that Scotland could – and should – govern itself led to the historic September 11, 1997 referendum – where the Scottish population voted in favor of a devolved parliament with the power to raise taxes.

The Scottish Parliament was thus established for the first time since the Act of Union in 1707. After the Conservatives lost all their Scottish seats, which were mainly swept up by the Labour Party, Prime Minister Tony Blair called for a referendum to assess the viability of re-establishing the Scottish Parliament. It would have control over Scotland's education and health care systems and was widely supported by the Liberal Democrats and the SNP. There were the expected growing pains, but the Scottish Parliament eventually evolved into a responsible legislative body that could defend Scottish national interests.

The growing thrust for Scottish independence and nationalism lead to the unexpected SNP victory in the 2007 elections. After half a century of political dominance, the Labour Party was displaced from their majority position in the Scottish Parliament. SNP leader Alex Salmond[138] became the first Nationalist to be elected First Minister of Scotland (i.e. the leader of the Scottish government) and went on to secure a second term in 2011. The following year, he secured the consent of British Prime Minister David Cameron to hold a referendum on Scotland's independence. Any Scottish citizen above the age of 16 was asked to answer a simple question on September 18, 2014: "Should Scotland be an independent country?"

Salmond argued that the Union no longer served Scotland's national interests, especially since the discovery of oil and gas reserves in the North Sea could help finance its economic independence from England. Proceeds from the tax revenue for oil could be used to create a sovereign fund (similar to Norway's) which would protect the welfare of its citizens for generations. On the other hand, the Scottish government's desire to retain the pound through a formal currency union with the rest of the United Kingdom was a highly contentious issue.

In the end, it appeared that a majority of Scottish citizens were not ready for the idea of an independent Scotland. 3.6 million Scots (approximately 85% of registered voters) made the trip to the polling booths. 51% of those who voted preferred to remain a part of the United Kingdom, while 49% opted to cut ties with England, Wales, and Northern Ireland.

Despite this unfavorable outcome, the SNP won the election for the Scottish Parliament for a third time in May 2016. First Minister Nicola Sturgeon[139] was tasked with the difficult question of considering Scotland's next move in light of the United Kingdom's decision to leave the European Union (i.e., Brexit)[140] on June 23, 2016. A significant majority of Scottish voters had opted to remain in the EU (62%), but the overall majority across England, Northern Ireland, Wales, and Scotland opted to leave (51.9%). An age-old dilemma had reappeared in a modern setting: should Scotland prioritize its ties to its southern neighbor or the wider European community at large?

As the Brexit negotiations intensify towards the United Kingdom's departure from the EU on March 29, 2019, Sturgeon's government appears to be intent on maintaining a strong economic and political alliance with the EU. It appears unlikely that Scotland will exit the UK in order to reapply for admission into the EU (this process could take years), so its best option is to maintain its position within the single market and customs union despite formally leaving the EU.[141] This would mean that Scotland would be able to export its goods to the rest of the EU without worrying about import taxes, embargoes, or levies, and that it would continue to adhere to the EU's uniform system for handling the flow of goods between member countries (no custom duties at borders between EU countries) and external nations (standard custom duties for goods from non-EU nations).[142]

Part 2: Wars of Scottish Independence

A Captivating Guide to the Battles Between the Kingdom of Scotland and the Kingdom of England, Including the Impact Made by King Robert the Bruce

Chapter 1 – Good Fences; Good Neighbors

The modern nation-state is by no means a universally applicable historical phenomenon; the Scotland of the 1200s had only recently arrived at a sense of a national identity. Alexander III,[155] who was the King of Scotland from 1249 to 1286, oversaw the policies that he had inherited from his predecessors. He relied mostly on a baronage system of Norman origins, which was conducted in French. (The Scots had embraced the fashions of European courts to gain more international clout and full acceptance within the community of West European monarchs).

The Scottish people lived a peaceful and prosperous existence under the same monarch for nearly four generations (who was lauded for governing "in love and law"), with a worldview more centered on local and regional loyalties than a sense of patriotism or nationalism. The term *Scotia*[156] was only applied to the entire kingdom north of England during Alexander II's reign (it had previously only referred to the lands north of the Clyde and Forth isthmus). The idea of "Scottishness" – like the ideas of Englishness, Irishness, and Welshness – is a relatively recent phenomenon. The boundaries between these four different bodies were not always clearly delineated.[157] In the past, parts of Scotland were ruled from Ireland, England, and Scandinavia, while parts of England and Ireland were ruled from Scotland.

The multiculturalism and multilingualism of Alexander III's diverse dominions reflected the psychical obstacles that stood in the way of a common sense of national belonging. Orkney and Shetland were constituents of the Scandinavian empire. The Inner and Outer Hebrides only entered the domain in 1266. Caithness and Sutherland were predominantly Norse; major parts of the north and west and Galloway (which was in the extreme south-west) were Celtic. Gaelic was still widely spoken in the Lowland counties of Ayr and Lanark. During this time, the Scottish language was slowly gaining eminence across the Lowlands. It originated in the southeast (from the Lothians and around Edinburgh), and would spread northward and westward throughout the twelfth century. It headed in multiple directions, on its way to becoming the lingua franca of Scotland: across the Forth and Clyde basins, westward to Kyle, southward to the Solway, and northward, past the Forth.

Berwick[158] may pale in comparison to Glasgow[159] and Edinburgh[160] (the state capital, now and then) today, but it was the most prosperous town and the center of Scottish trade with the Baltic and the Low Countries at the time. (Scotland conducted far less trade with England than it did with northern Germany and Scandinavia). Berwick was compared to Alexandria for its large population and immense wealth; its annual customs revenue was estimated to amount to one-quarter of England's. The stereotype of the Scottish as a "barbaric" and largely tribal people persists today, but the rule of David I[161] had "tamed" the wild nature of the Gaelic-Norse tribes and introduced the genteel influence of Christianity to the realm. The commissioning of majestic abbeys, monasteries, and churches reflect the growing eminence of the Scottish Church throughout this time. Under his just governance, people with different languages and customs were able to live together in peace and harmony.

The birth of the modern West European state occurred between the twelfth and thirteenth centuries. It was characterized by fully institutionalized administrative and legal systems, representation in parliament, a clearly defined national sovereignty, a commercialized economy, and a common vision of nationhood.[162] By 1100, England had developed all of these characteristics under its new Norman rulers and emerged as the most powerful political force in the British Isles. Wales and Ireland were the first political entities to feel the weight of its influence and power. Scotland's ability to defend itself against repeated English attempts to remove its sovereign identity prevented the vision of a fully English kingdom across the entirety of the medieval British Isles to be accomplished.

Scotland's ability to resist English conquest can be attributed to how it was able to absorb novel influences, technologies, and ideas and reshaped them for its own purposes. Scotland was open to colonists from England, Normandy, Brittany, and Flanders, thus exposing itself to the same ideas and political, religious and socio-economic changes that had brought about the "Europeanization of Europe."[163] After 1100, nearly every single important development in Scotland was derived from modes and resources that had been established beyond its own borders.

Despite its peaceful coexistence with England up until Alexander III's death, Scotland had been victimized by England's expansionist ambitions. The borders between the two kingdoms had been clearly defined. Scottish kings had long harbored the desire to reclaim Cumbria and Westmorland, which had once belonged to the southern portions of the kingdom of Strathclyde and the old kingdom of Northumbria. The position of Scotland in relation to England had been nebulous since the tenth century, when Scotland had relied on English aid to oppose the Danes. The English ruler had then been defined as "father and lord" of the King of Scots.

This led to an ironic and complicated reality where Scottish kings were also English magnates that owned titles and estates in England (often due to cross-border marriages). Since William the Conqueror[164] ruled Scotland, Scottish kings had to do homage for the English fiefs they held. The act of homage was never precisely defined – it involved a ceremony that was performed for the granting of land. This ceremony represented the submission of a vassal to his lord (which had to be there in person). The vassal would remove his crown or helmet, put aside his swords and spurs, and kneel before his lord. He would then stretch out his hands, which the lord would grasp. He would then proclaim: "I become your man from this day forth, of life and limb, and will hold faith to you for the lands I hold." After the act of homage and the oath of fealty, the lord and vassal would partake in the ceremony of investiture. The obligations that accompanied the act of homage were not explicitly stated, but they served as a powerful moral sanction for more specific responsibilities and engagements.

The Treaty of Falaise[165] in 1174 provides a sense of the relative positions of both Kingdoms. William the Lion had been captured by the English army, and would only be released if he agreed to pay homage to Henry for the Scottish crown. These terms were nevertheless cancelled after fifteen years, when Richard the

Lionheart[166] decided to sell the rights that his father had acquired to pay for his ventures in the Holy Land. This new agreement annulled the Treaty of Falaise, leaving the implications of homage as open-ended as it had been prior to 1174.

One of David I's legacies included the institutionalization of a strict form of kingship that depended on royal succession. This perpetuated a national monarchy and saved Scotland from the disruptions and costs of prolonged competitions for the throne. Alexander III thus succeeded the throne as a 7-year old in 1249 without any contestation. His long reign rested on the presumption that the Scottish kingship was equal in power and sovereignty to the English kingship; the Scottish kings also sought to obtain the pope's approval of the Scottish crown as a God-ordained anointment. In 1278, Alexander III was pressured to subject himself to Edward I. He confidently declined: "No one has the right to homage for my kingdom save God alone."

Chapter 2 – Crisis

As King Alexander III's long reign drew towards an end, Edward I was wrapping up his conquest of Wales. After six years of battle, he secured a victory in 1283. Two years later, he headed to Paris to pay homage to the new French king, Philip the Fair. [167] He remained there for three years, apparently confident of his power over England and Wales. While he was away, many prominent English ministers and judges became impossibly corrupt. Edward I was forced to return in 1289, and he decided to use the Jews as a scapegoat for the economic tumult and political chaos of the time. They were all expelled from England (a dangerous precedent for the rest of Europe), but all of their property and wealth remained, to be absorbed by the English state. Now flush with funding, Edward turned his expansionist gaze towards Scotland.

If Alexander III had heeded the prophecy of Thomas the Rhymer[168] (Sir Thomas Rymour of Ercildoune), there would have been an entirely different history written. The soothsayer had already predicted his imminent death, but Alexander decided to make the ill-advised decision to ride home during a storm at night. On 18 March 1286, he was attending a council in Edinburgh Castle. Instead of spending the night there after enjoying a good meal and fine wine with his barons, he decided to head home that night. This was presumably motivated by love or lust for his young French wife, Joleta of Dreux. At twenty-two, she was half his age. Alexander III had recently remarried after his first wife, Princess Margaret of England, died in 1275. The entire kingdom had been hoping for news of a healthy male heir. (Alexander's two sons had died before him, in 1281 and 1284).

Instead, everyone mourned when they heard that the king had been found dead, at the rocks at the foot of the cliffs. In the darkness and deafening howl of the winds, he had been separated from his two local guides and three esquires. The only surviving offspring was his granddaughter, Margaret of Norway.[169] Her mother had died during childbirth, leaving her under the care of her husband, King Eric II of Norway. [170] Two weeks after Alexander's death, Margaret was sworn in as the sovereign lady of Scotland. Six Guardians of Peace were elected as regents: two earls, two barons, and two bishops.

The Guardians of Peace maintained an uneasy peace for the next three years. By then, rivaling powerful factions had appeared, each with their own intentions for the empty throne. On 18 July 1920, the Guardians signed The Treaty of Birgham.[171] Its intentions were to maintain the peaceful coexistence between Scotland and England by having Margaret of Norway marry Lord Edward (the then-five-year-old son of King Edward I) when both royal children were of age. The two kingdoms would nevertheless remain separate; Margaret was to be hailed as Scotland's "true lady, queen and heir." In the Treaty, Edward I acknowledged Scotland's identity as a fully developed state that was "distinct and free from the realm of England," with its own "rightful boundaries" and "laws, liberties, and customs."[172] Edward was, however, harboring intentions to exert influence over his northern neighbor through his son's marriage. Everyone's intentions came to nothing, however, when Margaret died due to seasickness while sailing from Norway to Scotland. A direct, uninterrupted lineage of Scottish monarchs had come to a tragic end.

No less than thirteen candidates laid out their claims for the throne, each arguing that they were blood descendants of the Scottish royal family. Since Margaret's mother was dead, Eirik II of Norway no longer had a rightful claim to the throne. After the claims that were based on illegitimate offspring were dismissed, two main candidates for the throne emerged. They were John de Balliol[173] and Robert de Bruce.[174] Both men had large numbers of supporters and armed forces at their command. Scotland was poised to plunge into a disastrous civil war.

The Guardians of Scotland decided to invite Edward to adjudicate both men's claims, on account of his status as the King of England and his renowned legal expertise. Edward had a formidable reputation as an effective king. After he was crowned in 1272, he successfully corrected the legacy of his father, Henry III.[175] A reign characterized by internal strife and military impotence gave way to peace and military might. Edward had successfully negotiated peace between the warring English barons and demonstrated his prowess as a leader on the battlefield. He was also an intellectual with novel ideas on how he could successfully reform the English administration and government. Under his oversight, the Parliament maintained stability while collecting copious amounts of taxes from the English population. Whatever they felt towards Edward, the Scots would have to concede that he was a formidable opponent. After he died in 1307, they began referring to him as "Scottorum malleus": the Hammer of the Scots. (His nickname in life was "Longshanks" for his outstanding height).

Instead of concurring with Scotland's understanding of English overlordship as a matter of the distant past, Edward boldly proclaimed his overlordship over Scotland in the presence of the Scottish nobles and clergy on 10 May 1291. He argued that this would justify his appointment as adjudicator of who was the rightful ruler of Scotland. He then gave the Scottish nobles three weeks to put together a rebuttal after they vigorously objected to this shocking plot twist. During this time, he started assembling an army for the highly probability of a military skirmish.

The Scottish nobility were certainly more self-serving than they were patriotic or nationalistic. Many of them owned titles to large swaths of land in England, and were not willing to sacrifice those assets for the sake of national independence. *All* of the competitors for the Scottish throne soon decided to accept Edward's position as Lord

Paramount of Scotland. They would agree with his decision on who was the rightful ruler of Scotland. Edward carefully had each competitor write down this acknowledgment and stamp the document with their official seal. He also had every Scottish castle in the kingdom temporarily surrendered to him and replaced all Scottish officials with Englishmen. Every Scottish magnate, knight, freeman, and religious leader had to swear their loyalty to him by 27 July or endure harsh penalties.

John Balliol was eventually crowned King of Scotland in December 1292:

"As it is admitted that the kingdom of Scotland is indivisible, and, as the king of England

must judge of the rights of his subjects according to the laws and usages of the kingdoms

over which he reigns; and as, by the laws and usages of England and Scotland in the

succession to indivisible heritage, the more remote in degree of the first line of descent is

preferable to the nearer in degree of the second line; therefore it is decreed that John

Balliol shall have seisin of the kingdom of Scotland[176]."

Edward's decision to favor John Balliol was logical, since he was descended from a royal sister that was older than Robert Bruce's descendant. (Bruce had countered Balliol's claim by noting that he was one less generation removed from the royal lineage. He was the son of David I's great-granddaughter, while Balliol was the grandson of another great-granddaughter). It is nevertheless likely that he also had ulterior motives in favoring Balliol. Since he possessed significant amounts of land in the North of England, he had more to lose from defying Edward. Once Balliol was crowned King of Scotland, Edward was quick to assert his powers of overlordship. Scotland was now under English occupation in disguise.

The Scottish earls, knights, dukes, and magnates may have consigned themselves to the new status quo to protect their own interests, but the common people had little to gain – and much to lose – from meekly accepting the constant presence of the English military forces in their everyday lives. They were a proud people who felt humiliated by the easy, dishonorable way in which their elites had simply surrendered control of the nation to the English. Incidents of defiance and resistance soon gave way to brawls and riots in various Scottish towns and villages. A knight named Sir Malcolm Wallace died in one such conflict, leaving his son with a deep resentment towards the English that would remain with him until the day he died. His name was William Wallace.[177]

Chapter 3 – Defiance

The exact circumstances of William Wallace's origins are difficult to pin down, but his final resting place – in the hearts and minds of generations of proud Scottish patriots – is well known. Long before the rest of the world became acquainted with the legend of William Wallace via Mel Gibson's 1995 film *Braveheart*[178] (Gibson directed and starred in the Oscar-studded blockbuster), the citizens of Scotland had become familiarized with his outsized accomplishments through the work of fifteenth-century Scottish royal court poet Harry the Minstrel (or "Blind Harry ").[179] Blind Harry's *The Actes and Deidis of the Illustre and Vallyeant Campioun Schir William Wallace* (Acts and Deeds of the Illustrious and Valiant Champion Sir William Wallace, also known as *The Wallace*) was published nearly two centuries after Wallace's death.[180] The epic "romantic biographical" poem eventually became the second most popular book in Scotland after the Bible – a position that it retained for hundreds of years.

Before he made the meteoric rise to become a national icon, military legend, and patriot of the highest order, Wallace was the younger son of a minor nobleman. While he was never deprived of food, shelter, or an education, he also had no land titles to his name. Wallace lived his early life in what was termed the Scottish "golden age." Scotland enjoyed low taxes, bridges, good roads, and a thriving agricultural and cattle industry that surpassed even the English at the time.

When King Henry III of England died his son Edward, I took the throne. Edward was to be Wallace's most powerful opponent in the coming decades. While not having the same build as Wallace, Edward was nonetheless also known for his remarkably tall stature and deemed "Long-shanks." Wallace's adult height – a staggering two meters (six foot seven inches), at a time when the average adult man was only slightly taller than five feet – is testament to his exceptional genetics and the prosperity of his era. Blind Harry heaped poetic praise on his physique, singling out his wavy brown locks, sturdy neck, handsome facial features, broad shoulders, piercing eyes, and unmistakable "manly make."

At a time when close combat with sword or dagger were the common methods of physical dominance, Wallace's physical advantage would have served him well. However, without a keen mind to match he would not have reached the heights that made him figure of legend. Historians have speculated that he received an education from the monks in his area, learning to read and write. Wallace was also instructed in the manly arts of warfare, from riding to swordplay. He was trained in the use of a claymore (a two-handed sword) and also a dirk (a long slender dagger used for thrusting). Claymores were prodigious single warrior weapons at the time, taller than most men at six feet in length. Wallace's strength and a six-foot blade were more than enough to cleave through the armor available during his era.

In 1293, when Wallace was between eleven and thirteen years old, Edward I had just concluded his conquest of Wales after a six-year campaign. Edward then traveled to Paris to pay homage to France's new king; Philip the Fair. While away from England, Edward was confident in the knowledge that England and Wales were firmly under his control. Unfortunately, during his absence, many of his ministers and judges would sink to even greater depths of corruption. Edward returned to England in 1289 in the middle of political chaos and economic strife. He decided to expel all Jews from his kingdom, using them as a scapegoat for the current crisis. Once England had settled down, the ambitious leader then turned his gaze towards Scotland.

On 18th March 1286, King Alexander died. After attending a council meeting at Edinburgh Castle he decided to return home, but became separated from his escort and guides. He was found the next day, his dead body recovered from the rocks at the foot of the cliffs. After two weeks of mourning, Alexander's granddaughter, Margaret of Norway, was sworn in as the sovereign lady of Scotland.

Plans were made to marry Margaret of Norway to the son of King Edward I. The Treaty of Birgham was signed on 18 July 1286, effectively uniting the two royal members whilst still keeping England and Scotland separate. It was Edwards's intention to exert his influence on Scotland through his new daughter-in-law, however both his plans and the hopes of Scotland died with Margaret when she succumbed to sickness while at sea while traveling from Norway to Scotland.

Of the thirteen candidates for the throne after Margaret's death, two emerged with serious consideration; John de Balliol and Robert de Bruce. Since each man was backed by their own forces, Scotland appeared to be on the cusp of civil war. In the meantime, Edward, proffering advice and aid during Scotland's succession period, secretly met with his privy council to reveal his plans to subdue Scotland.

Unfortunately for Scotland, Edward I was a supremely able and effective leader. He inherited a throne fraught with internal instability after the passing of his father in 1272, and since his accession he had negotiated peaceful relations between England's restless barons, uniting them under his rule. His methods, while not always considered ethical, were highly effective. His skills also extended to raising funds, encouraging his Parliament to collect large amounts of taxes from the population. In 1275, he imposed the highly popular Statute of the Jewry, forcing exorbitant taxes on the Jewish population of England. By 1290 all Jews were expelled from the country, with all their financial assets confiscated by the crown. His financial prosperity thus positioned him in a favorable condition to begin a campaign north, into the lands of Scotland.

Meanwhile in Scotland, with the two factions of John de Balliol and Robert de Bruce threatening civil war, the guardians of Scotland decided to invite Edward I to adjudicate the many claims to the

Scottish throne. On 10 May 1291, King Edward proclaimed his rule over Scotland. In front of an assembly of Scottish nobles and clergy, Edward exerted both his position as an adjudicator and a "legitimate claimant" of the throne. He allowed three weeks for the gathered noblemen to formulate a rebuttal, yet he would use those weeks wisely, marshaling his armies and preparing for military action.

Most of the Scottish noblemen had lands and estates in English territory and knew well that they would be lost should they refuse Edward. All claimants for the throne eventually conceded to Edward's proclamation, naming him as Lord Paramount, accepting his judgment. Edward wasted no time, ordering that every Scottish castle be surrendered to him temporarily, and that all Scottish officials and judges be replaced by Englishmen. All nobility of Scottish descent, including knights, freemen, and religious leaders were to swear to Edward by 27 July or face harsh consequences.

Wallace was on the cusp of manhood (between seventeen to eighteen years old) when his father refused to administer his oath to Edward as Lord Paramount of Scotland. To escape the severe penalties that followed from this decision, he was forced to head northward with his father. His previous plans to embark on a lifelong career as a priest were thus permanently disrupted. While in hiding, his father was embroiled in a sporadic uprising of the Scottish villagers and townspeople against the imperious English soldiers (a fairly common occurrence, since the common people resented their interference in their everyday lives). Sir Malcolm Wallace was killed in one of these riots, leaving behind a son who would always harbor an intractable resentment towards the English.

The specific details may have been lost to time, but it is evident that Wallace's transformation into a feared guerrilla leader began not long after he endured the loss of his father. By 1291, Wallace was actively seeking ways to avenge his father and help his countrymen regain the upper hand against the English. Wallace's first high-profile target was the twenty-year-old son of Selby, an English constable serving under Baron Brian Fitz-Alan of Bedale. In response to the arrogant Englishman's taunts, Wallace stabbed him in the heart and wounded his comrades as he made for a quick escape. His brazen defiance soon earned him notoriety as an outlaw. To get around as a wanted man, he began wearing disguises (e.g. as a pilgrim) and spending more time in the safety of the Scottish woods.

Wallace was not alone in his defiance. King John Balliol resented Edward's interference in the country's national affairs and his status as a puppet figure. Edward had made him repeat his homage several times – a humiliation that was witnessed by the majority of nobles in the land. Edward angered King John further when he began interfering in the decisions made by Scottish courts. He deemed this a violation of the Treaty of Birgham, which mandated that all Scottish lawsuits should be adjudicated in Scotland. Edward then coerced him into acknowledging that the Treaty was now void – which thus established a troubling precedent where anyone could appeal to the English courts when the Scottish courts arrived at an unwanted decision.

King John seized the opportunity to retaliate when Edward got a taste of his own medicine in October 1293. King Philip of France was then in the enviable position of being England's feudal superior. After several English sailors went on an ill-advised rampage at the La Rochelle port, he ordered for all trade between the two countries to be halted. Edward responded by declaring war against France in October the following year. While Adolf of Germany remained neutral, France allied itself with Eirik II of Norway and Florence of Holland. Edward was preoccupied with a rebellion in Wales at the time, and demanded that King John report to London by 1 September 1294 with his armed forces to support him. Instead, King John allied Scotland with France and Norway and openly defied Edward on the 22nd of October.

The Scottish and English forces both prepared for a northern confrontation after Edward ordered for all of King John's titles and properties in England to be seized. The Scots had an early victory at the English town of Carlisle. Since they could not break through its defenses, they burned down the homes of the English citizens who lived outside the town walls. They also pillaged the monasteries, churches and villages in the countryside before returning past the Scottish border.

Edward had Scotland pay a bloody price for these transgressions. Three thousand foot soldiers and five thousand horsemen descended on Berwick, Scotland's largest and most prosperous city at the time. The townspeople were massacred, raped, and burned without mercy and remorse – as an example to the entire Scottish population. Edward only decided to call off the slaughter when he saw one of his soldiers hacking a woman apart as she was giving birth. At least seventeen thousand Scottish townsfolk (Berwick had a population of approximately twenty thousand people) had perished in the process.

The people of Scotland were nevertheless an immensely prideful and hardy group – they were not easily cowed (even by such shocking acts of bloodshed and violence). They rallied behind King John in defying English rule. On the 5th of April, he formally renounced his allegiance to Edward. Scottish renegades pulled off counterattacks to avenge their fallen countrymen at Berwick. After rebuilding Berwick, reinforcing it, and designating it as the new administrative center of his Scottish government, Edward launched his second attack against King John. The English army was then the most formidable military force in Europe, and the Scottish army did not stand a chance in a direct confrontation. Edward imprisoned 130 prominent Scottish knights, alongside a few earls and important magnates. His seamless victory crippled the Scottish victory, allowing the army to capture and seize control of all the major Scottish castles: Roxburgh Castle, Edinburgh Castle, and Stirling

Castle. By the 2nd of July, King John had formally surrendered and shipped off to England – where he was placed under a lengthy house arrest.

Before he left, Edward ripped out the royal Scottish insignia from his surcoat. Determined to stamp out all remaining symbols of Scotland's national identity, he also removed the Stone of Destiny (*Lia Fail*). This was the legendary basalt stone where every Celtic Scottish king had been crowned since the sixth century. After he arranged for himself to be crowned on the stone at Scone, he shipped it to Westminster Abbey alongside Scotland's crown jewels. They were only returned to Scotland in 1996. Edward also spirited away three chests that contained decades of royal records and important archives, which were never to be found again.

An all-important parliament session was held at Berwick on 28 August 1296. The agenda of the day was for all of Scotland's important bishops, earls, barons, abbots and priors to pledge their loyalties to him. Edward did not claim the title of King of Scotland for himself, however. Instead, everyone present paid homage to him as the King of England, Lord of Ireland and Duke of Guyenne. With John Balliol out of the picture, Robert Bruce, Lord of Annandale, was hoping to be named as his successor to the Scottish throne. After all, he had allied himself with Edward throughout King John's rule (and brief defection). Having had to exert himself to quash a rebellion, Edward was not interested in enshrining another figurehead. Satisfied with his grip over the country, he left Scotland a mere eleven days after the ceremony. He had to attend to more pressing matters that involved France. The bulk of the English army returned home when winter came, leaving a few garrisons behind to retain control of all of Scotland's castles.

Chapter 4 – The Martyr

Life under English rule was harsh and degrading for the common Scottish people. The English soldiers lorded over all the important Scottish castles and fortresses. They patrolled the countryside each day, ready to flex their military might and superiority complex against any man or woman who was deemed to be lacking in humility and subservience. The just rule of law was suspended in favor of exorbitantly harsh punishments for minor offenses. Scotsmen were flogged, mutilated and hung for mere misdemeanors. The mortality rate in the 1290s was thus exceptionally high.

Without a legitimate legal system in place, many people were forced to take matters into their own hands, some becoming brigands and forming robber bands to exact some measure of justice upon the English soldiers who freely roamed their countryside. English historians were quick to denounce the actions of the Scottish population, lamenting the atrocities committed against English soldiers. Rather hypocritically on the part of the historians, the barbarisms committed by the English soldiers against the Scottish population were not equally subject to condemnation.

Given these circumstances, it is not surprising that news of Wallace's exploits were greeted with much enthusiasm and awe during this time. Blind Harry's epic poem preserves the adulation of Wallace as the equivalent of Nottingham's Robin Hood, a charismatic outlaw that served an inspiring brand of vigilante justice to the English soldiers.

One such instance recorded in Blind Harry's epic poem details a challenge taken up by Wallace which had been put forth by an English soldier/weightlifter in the town of Ayr. Boasting of English superiority, the Soldier challenged any Scotsman to strike him across the back. Wallace, while in disguise, accepted the challenge and broke the English soldier's back with a single blow. He then quickly killed five other English soldiers before making his escape to Leglen Wood.

The Scottish people gained a measure of pride and awe in listening to (and repeating) tales of Wallace's small victories against the hated English. Around 1293, Wallace was transformed from a lone outlaw to a skilled militia leader. His swordsmanship and athletic prowess improved, as did his leadership skills and acumen as a military strategist.

Wallace's reputation also began to take on mythic qualities during his lifetime – a factor that arguably compensated for his lack of wealth and noble standing in the ideas of the common people.[181] In one particular skirmish in the town of Aur, Wallace nearly died after killing one of Lord Percy's men. Unable to escape from the overwhelming number of English soldiers that accosted him, he was captured and starved in a dungeon. When it was time for his trial, a severe fever had put him in a deep coma. The English soldiers assumed that he was dead and left his body to rot in a heap of dung. Wallace would have perished if not for the care and cunning of his first nurse at Ellerslie. She pleaded with the English for a chance to give him a proper burial, and quickly staged a fake wake to keep up the pretense that he was dead when she discovered that he was still alive.

After she nursed him back to health, Wallace gained a Christ-like reputation for having "returned from the dead." His fame grew when Thomas the Rhymer – a renowned prophet and soothsayer who had predicted Alexander III's death – learned that he was miraculously alive and prophesied that he would play a crucial role in restoring Scottish pride:

"For sooth, ere he decease,
Shall many thousands in the field make end.
From Scotland he shall forth the Southron send,
And Scotland thrice he shall bring to peace.

So good of hand again shall ne'er be kenned."[182]

In an age of superstition and destiny, Wallace had effectively turned into a magnetic larger-than-life figure. Men from all walks of life flocked to his side, turning the lone outlaw into a charismatic militia leader. He inspired faith, loyalty, and devotion in the band of brothers, nephews, uncles, cousins, and distant relatives that formed a tightly-knit military force around him. Motivated by the strength of large numbers, Wallace began to defy Edward's rule more brazenly.

In 1297, Wallace finally seized the opportunity to avenge his father's death. He successfully ambushed Fenwick, the English knight who had killed his father, after learning that he had returned to execute a mission in Scotland. By now, Wallace and his men had the benefit of more sophisticated weaponry: a steel helmet, armor for the torso and hands, a habergeon, and a steel collar. Wallace and his fifty men forced Fenwick – who was accompanied by one hundred and eighty men – to fight them on foot by stabbing the English horses under their bellies. Fenwick and his lieutenants were swiftly butchered, but eighty English soldiers managed to escape. (Wallace only lost three of his men). Wallace's army then claimed two hundred horses and the provisions they were carrying, along with the fallen English knights' weapons, armor, and money.

The news of this victory inspired many Scottish men and fugitives to join Wallace or resist the English in their own way. The English knights' reputation of invincibility had been punctured. Lord Percy initially attempted to establish a truce with Wallace (many Scottish magnates had switched sides after being lured by the promise of large estates and wealth). Wallace's uncle, Sir Ranald Crawford, managed to convince him to accept the truce presented to him. However, Wallace proved incapable to adapting to a life of peace and quiet after disbanding his army. After a bloody confrontation with English soldiers in town and the murder of several of Lord Percy's own men (they impertinently demanded that Wallace hand over Sir

Ranald's pack horse), Wallace was formally declared as an outlaw and an enemy of King Edward.

After recruiting sixty hardened men, Wallace began to emulate Robin Hood. His men began robbing and killing English knights and dispersing their possessions to the Scottish people. They took on Sir James Butler of Kinclaven and his men, once again nullifying the advantage of their horses and superior armor by forcing them to fight on foot. Wallace's victory streak was only disrupted by Sir Gerard Heron's thousand-man cavalry. Wallace's men were formidable in close combat, but they were easy targets for the English archers and their ample supply of arrows. After losing many of his men and suffering an arrow to his own neck (which left a lasting scar), Wallace was forced to retreat.

The most recent and well-known depiction of the tale of William Wallace is found in the 1995 Hollywood blockbuster film Braveheart. In this adaptation of the legend of Wallace, the love interest Murron MacClannough is introduced. Her attempted rape and murder further inspired Wallace to lead a revolt against the English. Although this addition of a lover further endows the tale of William Wallace with poetic justice, the original tale of Wallace by Blind Harry makes no mention of a Murron MacClannough. The original poem does, mention a woman named Innis who was credited with helping him escape from English troops, but there is no indication that she was either his wife or lover.

While the film does draw upon a love story as the initial motivation for Wallace's rebellion, the source is not entirely inaccurate. In a 1570 revised edition of Blind Harry's poem an eighteen-year-old, Marion Braidfute, is introduced as William Wallace's wife. In this edition, the motivations for Wallace's rebellion begin with the murder of Marion by the Sheriff of Lanark.

The poem's plot is simple and symbolic. Wallace meets Marion at an early age, falling in love with her at first sight at the Church of Saint Kentigern, near Lanark. Wallace began seeing Marion in secret, as their love during a time of civil unrest and war was seen as imprudent. To further complicate matters, the Sheriff of Lanark is, at the time, interested in Marion as a potential wife for his son.

The story continues as William Heselrig, Sheriff of Lanark, insults Wallace one Sunday morning as he is leaving Saint Kentigern's Church, leading to a fight between the English soldiers accompanying the Sheriff and Wallace's men. Wallace, having reportedly already married Marion in secret by this time, takes refuge in her home after retreating. A group of English soldiers accompanied by the Sheriff of Lanark marches to Marion's home and demands William's surrender. Marion buys enough time for William to escape out of a back window, however, once the Sheriff realizes that he had been tricked, he storms the home of Marion with his men and murders her in a rage.

Many historians argue that the addition of Marion was a result of a noble family's attempts to claim a link between their ancestry and Wallace's, with Marion having conveniently given birth to a daughter prior to her death at the hands of the Sheriff. The 1570s revision of Blind Harry's poem indicates that Wallace and Marion did manage to marry in secret and produce a daughter prior to her murder. The daughter subsequently married a squire named Shaw, thus preserving Wallace's lineage.

Several historians have dismissed all claims of the existence of Marion, claiming Wallace to have had no heirs, illegitimate or otherwise.

Whether the existence of Marion, or Murron, was fact or fiction, historians do confirm that Wallace successfully murdered the Sheriff of Lanark in May 1297. The night of the supposed murder of Marion, Wallace and his men returned to town, battling their way through the town's defenses and reportedly killing as many as 240 Englishmen. Wallace himself made straight for Heselrig's rooms, finding him and dispatching him with a single cut from his skull right down to the collarbone. After dealing with the Sheriff, he moved on to kill his adult son and then burned the family's house to the ground.

Though the motives may still be questioned, the killing of the Sheriff of Lanark was supported as truth in Wallace's trial documents. His charges at the trial noted the murder of the Sheriff as a symbolic action, one which galvanized the existing various resistance efforts into the first Scottish War of Independence.

After the massacre of Lanark, Wallace rallied his forces in Ayrshire, the territory he was most familiar with. Now in the company of old and new followers who were all under the spell of his revolutionary zeal, he had three thousand well-armed men at his disposal. His ranks included Gilbert de Grimsby (who was widely known as Jop), an esteemed soldier who had served in the English army and gained recognition from King Edward himself. With his formidable experience and critical intelligence regarding the English army, he was made Wallace's standard-bearer immediately. Wallace also had the support of Robert Wishart (the Bishop of Glasgow) and James the Steward, who had both been elected Guardians of Scotland in 1286. Wishart was opposed to Edward's attempts to anglicize the Scottish Church and was happy to support Wallace with his network of like-minded clergymen, the cover of the church, and his ability to "justify" Wallace's revolt as a legitimate war in the name of King John.

Several other prominent Scottish figures also defected to ally themselves with Wallace's brave band of rebels. This included William Douglas "the Bold" and Robert Bruce, the future King of Scotland.[183] Andrew de Moray, scion of an influential northern family which had led a revolt against the English and united the entire Moray area against them, became another noteworthy ally. Emboldened by Edward's absence (who had placed the ineffectual Hugh Cressingham in charge of English interests in Scotland), Wallace planned an attack on Perth – the center of the English regime in Scotland. The English were forced to retreat into the castles as the Scottish army advanced, leaving Wallace and his men free to claim the spoils and terrorize the English in turn.

In response, Edward rallied an army of three thousand horsemen and forty thousand footmen. His decisive show of force prompted the Scottish magnates to surrender on the 7th of July, since they were unable to reach a consensus on the army's leadership structure – or to establish an effective chain of command. Wallace was left to attack Lord Percy's forces with the help of Moray and his rebel army. After killing over five hundred English soldiers, they emerged victorious. When August 1297 ended, Wallace had reclaimed a large majority of northern Scotland. Apart from the strongholds of Dundee and Stirling, the English military presence had been purged from the land, forcing Hugh Cressingham to write to Edward informing him that no funding could be taxed from Scotland and requesting further aid from John de Warenne, the Earl of Surrey and Edward's Governor in Scotland:

> *"Sire, at the time when this letter was made, nor previously, from the time when I left you, not a penny could be raised in your [realm of Scotland by any means] until my lord the Earl of Warren shall enter into your land and compel the people of the country by force and sentences of law"*

Edward ordered John de Warenne to provide support to the garrison at Stirling and to raise the siege at Dundee. Wallace was busy attempting to subdue the English forces at Dundee when he learned of a large English force, led by Warenne and Cressingham, moving northward towards Stirling.

Stirling is located in a strategically crucial position in Scotland. The castle itself was perched upon a large crag that overlooked the surrounding plains and was one of the most formidable in the British Isles. Stirling was the gateway to the highlands, and so retaking the castle was seen by the English as the first step in reestablishing control over the north.

Warenne was confident of an English victory, having a vastly superior force and it was assumed that Wallace's rebellion would end with defeat in battle or by negotiation. And yet history would name Stirling as the site of Wallace's most iconic military victory, where he apprehended Cressingham and John de Warenne's large English army.[184] Despite their vastly superior numbers, weaponry, and logistics, the English cavalry and infantry was fatally undermined by the narrowness of the Stirling Bridge. It was only wide enough to accommodate two horsemen traveling abreast; the 16,000-strong English army would take a few hours to cross over in its entirety, all the while being in a strategically disadvantageous position.

Warrene had expected Wallace and Moray to surrender without a fight and was surprised when the much smaller army set up on the opposing bank, refusing to admit defeat. For a few days, both forces faced one another, each unwilling to make the first move. Warrene sent across the river two Dominican friars to negotiate a surrender. They returned with this message:

> "Tell your commander that we are not here to make peace but to do battle, defend ourselves and liberate our kingdom. Let them come on, and we shall prove this in their very beards."

Overconfident and impatient, because a prolonged battle meant more military expenditures, Warenne finally ordered his troops to cross the bridge on the 11th of September.

The entire English force was to move across the narrow bridge and engage the enemy on the opposite bank. A suggestion was put forth by Richard Lundie, a Scottish noble who had switched allegiance. He urged the English to send a force of horsemen and infantry upstream, to the Ford of Drip, to provide protection to the rest of the army as it advanced across the river:

> "My lords, if we go on to the bridge we are dead men; for we cannot cross it except two by two, and the enemy are on our

flank, and can come down on us as they will, all in one front. But there is a ford not far from here, where we can cross sixty at a time. Let me now, therefore, have five hundred knights and a small body of infantry, and we will get around the enemy on the rear and crush them; and meanwhile, you, my Lord Earl, and the others who are with you will cross the bridge in perfect safety."

Cressingham interceded however, complaining that a large amount of money had already been spent to subdue the revolution. A swift victory was required, and the English army was to cross the river immediately.

When slightly more than half of the English army had reached the other side, Wallace and Moray activated their trap. The Scottish rebels charged down the causeway with their long spears, while their comrades crossed the river to block the bridge's north end. With the archers on the Scots' side of the river, the English could not rely on their deadly range. Cressingham was killed alongside five thousand English soldiers, elevating the Battle of Stirling to Scotland's most significant victory against the English army since the Dark Ages. With Andrew Moray fatally wounded, Wallace did not have to share the credit for the momentous victory.

Wallace was hailed as the leader and savior of Scotland and embraced by the commoners (his popularity amongst the Scottish nobles was not as forthcoming). After his success at Stirling, Wallace forced the English army at Dundee to surrender. He reclaimed control of Cupar Castle, but was unable to force the English out of Edinburg Castle, Dunbar Castle, Berwick Castle, and Roxburgh Castle. With the exception of such strongholds, he managed to force a large portion of the English army out of Scotland. He also defeated Earl Patrick, an important Scottish magnate that refused to switch allegiances (he also insulted Wallace for his lowly origins).

Once Earl Patrick had been defeated, Wallace was able to turn the tables on Berwick, a previously Scottish settlement which had defected following a defeat the previous year. Wallace led his troops into the settlement, turning the small village into a scene of brutal carnage. Soon after Berwick, Wallace led his men south into Northumberland and Cumbria. The population of Northumbria had recently witnessed the previously undefeated English army fleeing southward and quickly followed suit, evacuating the area with all available food and cattle, leaving nothing for the Scots to scavenge.

By the time Wallace's army had reached Cumbria, however, they demonstrated that they had learned from previous mistakes. They moved far more carefully, claiming all the food and supplies available in the area before returning to Northumberland. This left them strong and well-equipped.

Wallace had no intention of attacking the fortresses which housed the remaining English Garrisons in Scotland, however he made an exception at Carlisle. Carlisle Castle was located at a strategic point on the western entry of Scotland, one which could not be left in English hands if the Scots were to secure control of Scotland. Wallace sent a large force to surround the Castle, yet had no plans to assault it. The rest of his army was sent to Newcastle to burn the town of Ryton to the ground after its inhabitants taunted the Scots from across the Tyne, its citizens having never thought that the army would wade across the river to retaliate!

Over the course of weeks, Wallace rampaged through northern England, burning over seven hundred English villages. Wallace's forces killed thousands of people in their rage, and those who were left had no will to resist the Scottish invaders. Thus, the army had free reign to pillage hundreds of villages and towns, taking most of their food and possessions.

The Scottish dominance in northern England came to an end not long before Christmas, with the English leading a counterattack under Sir Robert De Clifford. Several thousand English foot soldiers killed over three hundred Scotsmen at Annandale. By the time the

English advance halted at Christmas, they had ten villages and towns. They had reclaimed the town of Annan and destroyed the church at Gisburn. Innocents on both sides of the Scottish border would suffer immeasurably in this time, as the Scotsmen withdrew to the north.

Wallace reached the height of his powers during late 1297 and early 1298, when he was knighted as the Guardian of Scotland. This honor gave him the power to act on behalf of the entire Scottish realm – with the backing and consent of the magnates. There were undoubtedly many magnates who were opposed to the idea of a young man without prestigious origins becoming their leader, but Wallace had already won the people's hearts and had the backing of a surprisingly successful army. The Scottish knights, earls, and barons had also discredited themselves with their notoriously shaky allegiances.

Unfortunately for Wallace, the Scottish earls were ultimately unable to provide him with their undivided support. Wallace attempted to unite the disorganized and divided kingdom, but many of Scottish nobles could not put aside their envy and wounded pride to accept that they had been outranked by a commoner – even for the greater good. They were nevertheless loyal enough to Wallace to remain absent from a parliament session that Edward called for on 14 January 1298. This absence marked them as public enemies of England, and served as a sign for how Edward's control over Scotland had been diminished.

Only death would put an end to Edward's ambitions to conquer Scotland. (He would come to be known as "Scottorum malleus" – the Hammer of the Scots - after his death).[185] Undeterred by the English earls' indignant stance towards the financial costs of all of his foreign invasions, he began raising money to mount a decisive counter-attack against Wallace. He mobilized the Welsh troops and assembled an army of fourteen thousand horsemen and one hundred thousand foot soldiers; the largest army to be amassed against the Scots thus far.

John de Warenne, anxious to redeem himself after the battle of Stirling Bridge, led the massive English force on to Roxburgh, securing a quick triumph. The sheer size of the army allowed for several other swift victories, with Berwick surrendering. It was only at Kelso that the presence of Wallace's own cavalry halted further progress into the hills. At Berwick, Warenne received communication from Edward that he was returning from France to take supreme command over the Scottish invasion. Warenne was instructed to stay put at Berwick until Edward arrived.

To his credit, Wallace made extensive preparations to prepare for his ultimate confrontation with England's military might. He organized Scotland into military districts and began conscripting all able-bodied Scottish males that were older than sixteen. He established a merit-based chain of command, doing away with the feudal hierarchies that privileged members of the landowning classes in the military. He placed ambitious and able common men in the clergy, law enforcement, and the administrative workforce. While the Scotsmen were generally eager to join the growing army of its legendary leader, Wallace still left prudent reminders as to the consequences awaiting those who ignored his conscription regulations. He had gallows erected in every town, village, and burgh.

Wallace also turned to the clergy in his mission for reform, appointing William de Lamberton, an earlier supporter of Wallace, as head of St. Andrews. With Lamberton in a position of power, Wallace removed all English priests from the clergy, purging the ranks of those men that had been placed there by Edward. Some of the English priests and nuns that were removed were killed in the process.

Two towns in the Lothians and Berwickshire were destroyed to prevent the English access to food and supplies when they arrived. Wallace's scorched earth strategy proved to be effective in thwarting Edward's large army (approximately 87,500 men), whose morale became crippled by hunger when English supply ships were compromised by itinerant weather and Scottish pirates.

Wallace also devised a new military formation; one designed specifically to combat the English heavy cavalry which was so effective against the lightly armored Scottish footmen. The tactic was named the schiltron. Foot soldiers would utilize twelve-foot long spears to create a hedgehog-like defensive formation, with spear points poised in all directions. With the foot soldiers also carrying shields, the Scottish infantry was in a better position to survive the English archers as well as the charge of the heavily armored English Knights.

Edward returned to England and began laying down his plans to invade the north, testing the strength of the Scottish defenses as well as the people's will to resist. Edward began moving up large quantities of supplies to Carlisle, with more supplies being amassed in England to be shipped to Berwick and Edinburgh once they were reclaimed. All this was in preparation of the main invasion which took place on 25 June 1298.

Edward arrived at Roxburgh on the 24 June to an army that was comprised of four thousand light horsemen, three thousand heavy cavalry, and eighty thousand foot soldiers. Of the eighty thousand foot soldiers, a majority of them were troops hired from Ireland and Wales. The English marched from Roxburgh to eventually engage Wallace's army at the Battle of Falkirk.

Edwards massive army came with massive logistical problems. Despite the supplies that had been prepared prior to the army's departure, feeding the army was still a laborious and difficult task. It was not made easier by Wallace's scorched earth strategy, which left the English nothing to forage while on the move into Scotland. Edward attempted to lift the morale of his troops by distributing two hundred casks of wine from supply ships that had managed to evade Scottish pirates. However, this simply led to infighting between the English and Welsh troops, further demoralizing the hungry army.

With the army suffering attrition and low morale, Edward ordered his troops to withdraw to Edinburgh to wait for supplies. It was at Edinburgh that Edward was informed of the sighting of the Scottish army, eighteen miles away in the forest of Selkirk. By 9 a.m. that day the English army was marching towards Falkirk, arriving at Linlithgow by nightfall. Scottish cavalry was spotted the next day, and the English army moved towards the fields of Falkirk.

Wallace would have had a longer political and military career if he had out-waited the English army longer. Instead of continuously eluding them in the Scottish countryside and waiting for them to retreat due to fatigue and acute food shortages, Wallace's army engaged Edward's men in an ill-advised direct confrontation at the Battle of Falkirk.

Wallace had the schiltron – his new military formation devised to confront the English cavalry. However, he could not have anticipated the deadly range of the Welshmen and Lancastrians' longbow. This recent military invention was as comparable to medieval warfare as poison gas had been to modern warfare.

Edward initially ordered the Welsh to advance against the Scottish schiltron. However, they refused to be used as guinea pigs, forcing Edward to instead order forth the English Cavalry. As the cavalry advanced, they found that the seemingly sturdy meadows were hiding swampy grounds. Unable to advance, the heavy cavalry was forced to find a way around the bog. The second line of cavalry advanced more warily, heading towards the eastern side of the swamp, awaiting the third advance line led by Edward himself.

Wallace's schiltrons were in a position to cover all four lines of the English cavalry; his footmen were disciplined and well-armed with their spears. The English cavalry was unwilling to directly confront this hedgehog-like formation, and so turned their attention to the Scottish archers.

While the cavalry made quick work of the Scottish archers, Edward ordered the advance of the infantry, including the Lancastrian bowmen, who let fly their arrows at incredible range. The Scotsmen simply had no defense against the ceaseless rain of arrows that showered down from the sky – accompanied by the flurry of stones and rocks hurled by the English infantry. As the once-impregnable schiltrons floundered under the endless hail of arrows and projectiles, Wallace's men abandoned their ranks to retreat. The English knights then rode them down, culling the men in close combat – where their twelve-foot spears were practically useless.

Wallace managed to escape with a few surviving members of his army. His infantry (which was once ten thousand men strong) had been massacred, but the Scottish cavalry had wisely decided to retreat and fight the English in more favorable conditions. Wallace's reputation as a military leader had been permanently maimed. He gave up his Guardianship of Scotland soon afterwards, and returned to life as an outlaw. During his retreat from the English army, he ordered for the towns of Stirling and Perth to be destroyed. When the supply ships Edward was expecting from Ireland and west England failed to arrive, the English army suffered from a fifteen-day famine. Edward was thus forced to abandon his plans to completely eradicate what remained of Scotland's resistance forces.

For the next seven years, Edward ordered his troops to attack Scotland annually. Wallace's life was largely anti-climactic during this time. He harassed the English whenever he could with his tightly-knit band of outlaws, while also occasionally traveling abroad to win the support of King Phillip of France, Eric II of Norway, and the Pope. Wallace's diplomatic efforts were ultimately unsuccessful. By 1304, the Scottish nobility surrendered and agreed to sign an agreement with Edward. After he accepted the submission of the Scottish nobility, Edward himself led an attack on Stirling Castle – the last stronghold that defied English rule.

Edward ordered the castle be blockaded, preventing supplies from reaching the defenders. Massive siege engines were shipped in from Edinburgh, and Stirling Castle's walls would be tested by the greatest artillery the English possessed at the time. On April 22, Edward took control of the siege operations at Stirling. The English siege arsenal was varied. For example, there were thirteen trebuchets each capable of hurling a stone weighing three hundred pounds over a thousand yards. There were other specialized machines used for pulling their own galleries and parapets, rams for tackling the gates, and even a mobile tower that was capable of lifting a cage of twenty men over the walls of the castle.

The defenders did not succumb without a fight, unleashing boiling oil and molten lead on the attackers. However, the lack of supplies was taking a toll. On 20 July 1304, the Scottish rebels finally succumbed to Edward's demand for an absolute and unconditional surrender. The leader of the rebels of Stirling, Sir William Oliphant, was imprisoned in the tower of London, leaving Wallace now as the lone figure in opposition to the English. With a bounty of three hundred marks on Wallace's head and Edward's determination to capture him, Wallace had no chance of victory and little chance of survival.

Edward was merciful to the Scottish magnates who opposed him, only offering public humiliation, banishment for a few years, or exile; he seemed only to harbor a hatred for Wallace. Edward forced Scottish leaders to hunt Wallace down in return for more lenient punishments for their insurrection. Despite the offer, none of these men took any serious action towards hunting down the legendary Scot.

Wallace was ultimately betrayed by his own servant, Jack Short, and Sir John Menteith, a trusted Scottish baron who had been tempted by Edward's promise of wealth and land titles. Edward specifically selected John Menteith to hunt down Wallace as the man knew him personally, Wallace being the godfather to Menteith's two sons.

In Blind Harry's epic poem, Menteith was apparently reluctant to execute his mission. It was only after he was written to personally by Edward that he arranged for his nephew to join Wallace's guerrilla band, to keep track of Wallace's movements. Wallace had ridden out of Robroyston, hoping to meet with Robert Bruce, the man he believed could restore Scottish independence whereas he could not. Menteith's nephew quickly informed him of the plan, and with sixty of his most loyal men he rode out to intercept Wallace's much larger force.

No fight was to occur between the two forces as Menteith waited for nightfall before coming upon Wallace's camp. Wallace's right-hand man was killed before Wallace himself was dragged from the bed he shared with his mistress. Hopelessly outnumbered, Wallace still attempted to fight off Menteith's men with his bare hands. Blind Harry mentions that Wallace was deceived, Menteith had stated that the area was surrounded by a much larger force than the one he had actually brought along. Naively, Wallace agreed to be bound hand and foot and escorted to Dumbarton Castle under the protection of Menteith.

For this Menteith was rewarded handsomely. Edward's note had requested that Menteith capture Wallace alive in order to allow for a humiliating death that would destroy the legend's reputation and further demoralize the defeated Scots.

After being captured, he was put through a show trial in Westminster and quickly found guilty of sedition, homicide, robbery, arson, and other crimes.

The trial was important for impressing upon both the English and Scottish the depravity to which Wallace had stooped in his ungodly insurrection against the English Crown. English propaganda had painted a picture of the gigantic young man as "an ogre of unspeakable depravity who skinned his prisoners alive, burned babies, and forced nuns to dance naked for him." Wallace's English reputation also extended to a torturer of priests, rapist of nuns, and murderer of women and children by fire and sword.

No opportunity for defense was given to Wallace, and he was given no lawyer nor any opportunity to speak against the charges laid against him. The murder of the Sheriff of Lanark by Wallace was singled out as the event catalyst which sparked the Scottish insurrection against the "rightful" lord of Scotland, Edward. Wallace did, however, make sure to loudly declare to all that could hear that he could not be guilty of treason, having never pledged allegiance to Edward.

Wallace was executed at Westminster on the 23 August 1305 as a large English crowd cheered on. Wallace's death was seen as fairly standard procedure for those found guilty of treason during this period.[186] Wallace was stripped naked before being led to the execution grounds. Drawn by horses, the naked Scot was led from the Palace of Westminster to the Tower of London and then through the city to the Elms. Garbage and excrement were thrown at him by jeering English crowds.

Once Wallace reached the Elms he was taken from the cart to the gallows. There he was hung but taken down before his neck could break. His genitals were removed and he was disemboweled, his intestines pulled out to be burned. His internal organs followed as the executioner removed liver and lungs. His final death came at the removal of his heart from his body. English mobs cheered as his head was cut off with a cleaver. All of this was intended to humiliate and degrade the Scottish hero. His body was then quartered; cut into four pieces.

His head was hung up on the London Bridge, while the four quarters were sent to Newcastle-upon-Tyne, Berwick, Stirling, and St. Johnson "as a warning and a deterrent to all that pass by and behold them." Edward intended for Wallace's fate to be a traumatic warning to anyone in Scotland who dared to resist his rule, but Wallace would prove to be more powerful in death than he had been in life. He lived on as a folk hero and a martyr of the highest order – an immortal symbol of the lengths and depths that Scotland was willing to go to free itself from the cursed yoke of English oppression.

Chapter 5 – Power Struggles

Wallace's legendary patriotic zeal – during and after his lifetime – may have inspired many Scottish elites to defect from Edward and believe in their ability to resist English rule, but he was never able to unite them. After Wallace's fall from grace, the Scottish nobility was still divided along the fault lines that had first appeared during Scotland's succession crisis.

After Wallace's career as the Guardian of Scotland ended, a fragile truce was established between two rival nobles: John Comyn and Robert the Bruce. Comyn was a nephew of John Balliol, the exiled King of Scotland. The Comyns were a powerful northern noble family with significant military resources, and were personally invested in arranging for the exiled King John to return to Scotland. Robert the Bruce shared the same name as his grandfather – who had competed with John Balliol for the Scottish throne in 1290 – and harbored similar royal ambitions.

By May of 1300, Bruce was unable to put up the pretense of supporting Balliol's return and resigned from the position of joint Guardian. By 1304, however, John Balliol had resigned himself to the fact that he would never be able to return to his throne. Scotland's diplomatic maneuvers had come to naught. The Pope needed Edward's military support for his latest crusade against Islam. After the death of his first wife Eleanor, Edward shrewdly arranged for his marriage to Marguerite – King Philip's seventeen-year-old sister – to broker a treaty of peace with France. King Philip and Pope Boniface ended up in an open war against each other, resulting in the Pope's death. As the de facto leader of the Scottish nobility, Comyn headed the peace negotiations with Edward on 9 February 1304. This capitulation was a death sentence for all hopes that Balliol would be restored to the Scottish throne. Bruce's own father also died in 1304 – leaving him as the sole claimant to the throne.

Two years and one day later, the single most decisive political murder in Scottish history occurred. John Comyn met Robert Bruce at the Greyfriars monastery in Dumfries, presumably on peaceful terms now that Edward's rule over Scotland had been formally accepted by all the nobles. It is also unclear if it was Robert Bruce or his followers which dealt the coup de grâce, but Comyn was left dead by a fatal knife wound on the church altar.

Bruce's intentions for killing Comyn remain murky, as does his legacy as *the* freedom fighter that finally secured Scotland's independence. When compared to Wallace's pure, unambiguous patriotism, Bruce certainly appeared to be far more opportunistic, self-serving, and calculative. (One should remember, however, that it was exceedingly common for Scottish nobles of the time to switch sides in order to pursue power). Bruce and his father had supported Edward I when he invaded Scotland in 1296, with hopes of securing the crown for their lineage after Balliol was displaced. During the tumultuous rebellions against English rule between 1295 and 1304, Bruce alternated between being one of Wallace's leading supporters and a trusted ally to Edward. Bruce had switched sides several times, being a Guardian of Scotland during a period of resistance, and then switching sides back to Edward during the loss of the battle of Falkirk. While Bruce's switching of sides can be considered inconsistent and fickle, his actions were similar to those of all other nobles with lands and estates, whose loyalties were to family and fortune first.

Under encouragement from Bishop Wishart, Bruce had raised the standard of revolt at Irvine in 1297. This meant his absence from the legendary Battle of Stirling Bridge. After his uprising failed and Wallace emerged victorious, Bruce did not join his ranks. Instead he maintained a low profile and waited to see how the English would respond to the unexpected defeat. Bruce had also been absent at the calamitous Battle of Falkirk.

There was thus no evidence from this time – and certainly no prophecy – that would suggest his eventual transformation into a leader of Scotland's war of independence. In any case, it is unlikely that Bruce murdered Comyn for any abstract ideals pertaining to Scottish pride and honor. Bruce ostensibly either (1) assassinated Comyn in cold-blood to pave the way to the throne; or (2) killed him out of rage – their rivalry had certainly incurred political and financial costs on his side – and then improvised a bid for the throne.

Historians are unsure of what transpired during that fateful meeting, but they are clear on the consequences of Comyn's death. Given Bruce's possible motives for killing Comyn, the Pope decided to punish him for committing murder in a holy place. Bruce was excommunicated (i.e. banished from the Catholic Church) for this sacrilege. This was a severe blow to Bruce's royal ambitions, as the Church would have conferred legitimacy and protection to his status as a rightful monarch. Undeterred, he proceeded to claim the throne for himself. Bruce did have the support of Robert Wishart, the Bishop of Glasgow and one of Wallace's key supporters. Wishart convinced Bruce to seize the throne and helped to organize his coronation. On the 25th of March, Bruce hastened to Scone and was crowned as the King of Scotland (the Stone of Scone and Scottish Crown Jewels were absent from the ceremony).

Bruce may have secured the throne with seemingly little effort, but his unexpected position was King was exceedingly difficult. Edward had firm control over the majority of Scotland's important castles and deemed him to be a traitor. Many of the other Scottish nobles had been allied to Comyn and John Balliol and did not attend Bruce's crowning ceremony. With a possible civil war on his hands and Edward's wrath on his head, Bruce's position was exceedingly precarious.

He did not have to wait long to suffer for his audacious royal ambitions. In June 1306, he endured his first defeat against Edward's army at the Battle of Methven. Led by Aymer de Valence,

2nd Earl of Pembroke,[187] the English force took Bruce's army by surprise and nearly eradicated it completely. Bruce escaped with a few followers towards his homelands in the southwest, leaving his two clerical supporters - William de Lamberton and Robert Wishart – to languish in an English dungeon. (Since they were holy men, they were spared from execution).

Bruce suffered from more personal and military losses even while he was traveling towards his lands. His own men were intercepted by John MacDougall and his men. A Comyn supporter, MacDougall was bent on revenge for John Comyn's murder at Greyfriars. Bruce was lucky to survive the Battle of Dalry in July 1306, which nearly eliminated all of his surviving supporters. Bruce was now practically a fugitive, hounded by the English and his Scottish opponents.

He was then forced to endure traumatic personal losses. His wife, daughter, and two sisters had been traveling with him and his men, but he decided to send them to Kildrummy Castle out of concerns for their safety. They were escorted by his younger brother Neil. In September, the English attacked the castle and forced the Scots to surrender. Neil was hung, drawn and beheaded (like Wallace) – a devastating blow to Bruce (the eldest brother) and his remaining three brothers (Edward, Thomas, and Alexander). The English also captured Bruce's wife, daughter, and two sisters and placed them under house arrest. As hostages, they could be useful pawns in a negotiation with Bruce if he ever rose to power. Mary Bruce and Isabella, the Countess of Buchan, were both imprisoned in cages that were hung from their respective castles (Berwick and Roxburgh) to deter other rebels.

Chapter 6 – Inner Strife

The fall and winter of 1306 was the lowest point in Bruce's career. [188] He was forced to flee from the Scottish mainland, and earned the unenviable nickname of King Hob ("King Nobody") during this time. His exact hideout during this trying period remains unknown, but historians speculate that he hid out in a cave on Rathlin Island, which lies between Kintyre and County Antrim in Northern Ireland. While Bruce was absent, the English captured two more of his brothers: Thomas and Alexander. Both were executed. Bruce is purported to have retained his hope and patience from watching a spider persevere in its seemingly futile and foolish attempts to spin a web from one area of the cave's roof to another (alternate versions of the story replace the cave's roof with two roof means). After failing twice, it achieved its objective on its third attempt.

In February 1307, Bruce returned to the Scottish mainland to face his opponents a third time. His primary supporter was Edward, his last surviving brother. Bruce and Edward gathered more supporters from their family lands at Carrick. After his early disasters, Bruce had reached the wise conclusion that he could never defeat the English in a traditional battle. Like Wallace, he stood the best chance by relying on ambushes, surprise attacks, guerrilla tactics, and unconventional military strategies:

"Let Scotland's warcraft be this: footsoldiers, mountains and marshy ground; and let her woods, her bow and spear serve for barricades. Let menace lurk in all her narrow places among her warrior bands, and let her plains so burn with fire that her enemies flee away. Crying out in the night, let her men be on their guard, and her enemies in confusion will flee from hunger's sword. Surely it will be so, as we're guided by Robert, our lord."

- *Scotland's Strategy of Guerrilla Warfare (c.1308)*[189]

In April, Bruce secured his first minor victory against the English with the Battle of Glen Trool.[190] His strategy of ambushing John

Mowbray and his men by charging down the steep hillsides proved to be highly effective. The following month, Bruce redeemed his military reputation by defeating Aymer de Valence at the Battle of Loudoun Hill. This time, Bruce gained the upper hand via the same "bottleneck" circumstances that had tipped the scale in Wallace's favor at the Battle of Stirling Bridge. Valence had the larger army, but his men were hindered by a large bog and the parallel ditches that Bruce's men had dug out.

Valence had been in charge of the main English force in Scotland. This victory undoubtedly boosted the hopes and confidence of Bruce and his supporters. It was more empowering, however, to learn the news of Edward I's death. While traveling with the aims of reconquering Scotland once and for all, he died at Burgh-on-Sands after falling ill near the Scottish border. His son and successor, Edward II, decided to head south to secure his position as the new King of England – instead of confronting Bruce. Edward II gave some of the highest offices in England to his father's most noteworthy opponents – which earned him much antagonism from the barons.

A large portion of the conflict between Edward II and the barons revolved around Piers Gaveston,[191] Edward II's former playmate and foster brother. Edward I himself was responsible for introducing his household to Gaveston. He was a few years older than Edward II, and was deemed a positive role model for his military prowess, athleticism, and good manners. By 1303, Gaveston was designated as *socious* (companion) instead of a *scutifer* (esquire). In 1306, both were knighted. However, Edward I banished Gaveston to France later that year for reasons that remain unclear.

Not long after Edward II was crowned, he made Gaveston his chief adviser and made him the Earl of Cornwall (a title that had only be conferred on royalty; Gaveston was the son of a Gascon knight). Gaveston was also granted huge grants of land, and the hand in marriage of Margaret de Clare, Gloucester heiress. The true nature of Edward II and Gaveston's unusually close relationship is difficult to ascertain. Some historians have argued that they had entered into a "brotherhood-in-arms," while others argue that they were actually lovers (some speculate that Edward I had banished Gaveston to make way for his son's marriage to Isabella of France).[192] It is nevertheless clear that Gaveston's "undue" wealth, position, status, and arrogance incited the jealousy and anger of the barons, Edward II's young wife Isabella, and his father-in-law King Philip of France. Chroniclers of the era lamented the king's love for Gaveston, which was described as "excessive," "inordinate," "immoderate," and "beyond measure and reason."[193]

Regardless of the true nature of their relationship, the idea and practice of royal favorites would not have been such a major cause for concern if Edward II had been an effectual leader.[194] He had inherited a costly Scottish conquest, and the English crown was heavily in debt. He was unable to raise an army to combat Robert the Bruce, but nevertheless taxed the English people and forcibly seized crops from them. Edward II was easily distracted, inept at military affairs, thoughtless, and weak. Instead of addressing pressing military and administrative matters, Edward was often hiding away in his chambers with Gaveston. By allowing the barons to become royal enemies instead of royal allies, Edward II sealed his place in history as the worst of England's Plantagenet kings.

In 1311, a baronial committee consisting of 21 members drafted the "Ordinances"[195] – a document that called for Gaveston to be permanently banished from England and for Edward II's powers over important appointments and finances to be restricted. It was passed in November that year, but Gaveston boldly defied it by returning to England in January the following year. Edward II publicly restored him, which enraged the barons. Thomas of Lancaster, Edward's cousin and the most powerful baron in landed terms, sentenced Gaveston to death after he was captured by baronial forces in 1312.

Instead of restoring the English government, however, Gaveston's death only lead to more civil strife. The English were divided between Lancaster supporters and those who felt that the murder was a breach of justice (even if they were happy to see Gaveston eliminated). Two other problematic figures which exerted a more negative influence than Gaverston ever did eventually appeared at Edward II's side as his new favorites: Hugh Despenser the Elder and his son, Hugh Despenser the Younger.[196]

Edward II's ineffectual leadership and drawn out, ultimately doomed campaign against the powerful English barons certainly worked in Bruce's favor, as it gave him more time to solidify his own position. Unlike his English counterpart, he would prove successful in bending the Scottish noble to his will. His first objective was to defeat John Comyn's supporters. As the English courts were embroiled in inner strife in the winter between 1307 and 1308, Bruce marched northeast towards the northern Comyn lands. He defeated the Earl of Ross and captured the castles in the Great Glen. He gained control of Inverlochy, Urquhart, and Inverness.

In 1308, Bruce journeyed eastwards towards the Comyn castles of Banff, Balvenie and Duffus in Buchan. He attacked the Black Isle despite being perilously ill. He successfully defeated John Comyn, the 3rd Earl of Buchan (the cousin of John III Comyn, which Bruce murdered at Greyfriars and Bruce's primary opponent), at the Battle of Inverurie in May. Bruce's men also defeated the English garrison at Aberdeen. To ensure that the Comyn family was thoroughly defeated, he ordered the Harrying of Buchan in 1308. Buchan was the agricultural hub of northern Scotland and a Comyn stronghold (support for the family was strong even after Comyn was defeated). Bruce had large swaths of farmland burned, livestock slain, and

Comyn supporters murdered. The Comyn castles in Moray, Aberdeen, and Buchan were ruined.

During the autumn of 1308, Bruce turned his sights on the MacDougall clan in Argyll, longtime allies of the Comyns in the southwest. After claiming Dunstaffnage Castle at the Battle of Pass of Brander, Bruce had successfully wiped out the MacDougall army and defeated the Comyn's final major stronghold. After controlling northern and southwestern Scotland for a century and a half, the Comyn family was obliterated. Bruce assumed control of the entirety of northern Scotland by March of 1309.[197]

Emboldened by his domestic victories, he called for his first parliament at St. Andrews that month. His position as the King of Scotland was supported by the remaining nobles and a letter from Philip of France. A year later, the Scottish bishops recognized his claim to the throne (despite his excommunication from the Catholic Church) in the Declaration of the Clergy - a document which absolved him of the sins of his past. Despite the Pope's interdict (which suspended all Church activities in Scotland following Bruce's excommunication), the Scottish bishops remained unflinching Bruce supporters. He was, after all, their only hope for the Scottish Church's separate existence and legitimacy (Bruce's defeat would mean endless interferences from the English Church).[198]

By 1310, Bruce no longer had to contend with opponents on his home soil. He turned his gaze southward, to the Lowlands that lay southwards of the River Tay – Scottish territory that was still under English control.

Chapter 7 – The Battle of Bannockburn

After failing to negotiate a truce with Edward II, Bruce began to forcefully recapture the Scottish castles and important outposts occupied by the English in the Lowlands. Linlithgow was reclaimed in 1310, Dumbarton in 1311, and Perth was won by Bruce himself in January 1312.[199] Despite being stepped in the code of honor and military tactics of a feudal knight, Bruce provided to be as effective (or more) of a guerrilla fighter as Wallace. Bruce even extended his military excursions into northern England, capturing Castle Rushen in Castletown and occupying the entire Isle of Man – an island of significant strategic importance to the English.

As Bruce continued to harass English troops and the northern English towns, his brother Edward Bruce surrounded Stirling Castle. By this time, it was the final key stronghold that still remained under English control. Its governor, Philip de Mowbray, held off the Scottish attackers, but agreed to surrender if reinforcements from Edward II did not arrive by the midsummer of 1314. Edward II received the news by May and hastened towards the key fortification from Berwick. His force – which consisted of approximately 3,000 cavalry and 13,000 infantry (including a contingent of Welsh archers) - reached the southward part of Stirling by the following month. This was the largest English army to have ever invaded Scotland. (Edward II had actually summoned 25,000 infantry from England, Ireland and Wales, but only half of them reported for duty).

Robert Bruce's force had already arrived, ready to compensate for their much smaller numbers (7,000 infantry and a few hundred cavalry). Most of Bruce's footmen were armed with pikes,[200] a long spear that consisted of a heavy wooden shaft (between 3 – 6 meters in length) and a leaf-shaped steel point. They were led by the King, his brother Edward, and his nephew Sir Thomas Randolph (the Earl of Moray).[201] Each leader was in command of a single division of schiltrons. Eight years of victorious guerrilla warfare against the

English and their Scottish opponents had shaped Bruce's men into an experienced and tough fighting force.

Bruce assembled his men at the New Park: a royal hunting preserve that lay between 1-2 miles (1.6 – 3.2 km) south of Stirling. His strategy was to use the tree formations there to funnel the English army directly towards his heavily armed footmen and recently excavated anti-cavalry ditches. When the English army arrived on June 23rd, his traps were ready. The road to Stirling was blocked by the Scottish army, prompting the English to meet the Scots on disadvantageous terrain.

On the 23rd June, Edward II sent out two different scouting parties to survey the area before his main force advanced further. The party led by the Earl of Hereford stumbled upon Bruce himself, as he was inspecting the strength and numbers of the English troops. An English knight named Henry de Bohun charged directly towards Bruce. (If he successfully killed or captured Bruce, he would receive a lifetime of praise as a war hero). After quickly sidestepping Bohun's lance, Bruce killed him with a single blow of his battle axes (to the back of the head). Hereford was then forced to retreat back towards the English camp by Bruce's supporters. Meanwhile, the Earl of Moray and his schiltron fought back the rest of the advancing English forces. Two of Edward II's experienced commanders, Sir Henry Beaumont and Sir Robert Clifford, were forced to retreat after a violent confrontation. Without the Welsh archers, the English knights were ill-equipped to confront the Scots' formidable thicket of spears. Their swords and maces were useless against the advancing schiltrons, which moved forward slowly and eventually forced them to take flight. (This offensive use of the schiltrons was a new tactic; Wallace had only used them as a form of static defense).

The Scots thus emerged the victors on the first day of the Battle of Bannockburn. Edward II decided to relocate his army closer to the banks of the Bannock-burn that evening (out of fears that Bruce would attack them in the night). This was an inevitably unhelpful decision, as his men suffered from poor sleep on the wet and marshy grounds.

The next morning, the Scottish army assumed their planned battle formation against a sleep-deprived and disorganized English force. The English nevertheless hoped to restage Wallace's defeat at the Battle of Falkirk. In a full-scale direct confrontation, Welsh longbowmen would be able to take on the Scottish schiltrons in a clean sweep. To Edward II's delight, Bruce decided to risk everything and face the English in an open battle. This was no reckless decision. At this critical point in time, a Scottish noble in the English army had switched sides and brought crucial intelligence to Bruce. Sir Alexander Seton reported that the English were suffering from low morale. He also revealed their confined position.

Even if the circumstances were fortuitous, the Scottish army was still taking on a grave risk. To be on the safe side, Bruce had planned for a strategic retreat if the outcome of the battle was not in his favor. The judgment of God was deemed to be a critical factor in such medieval battles (this is why the Scottish's clergy's decision to pardon Bruce's transgressions was so important). In the heart of one of the Scots' schiltrons, Abbot Bernard of Arbroath held tightly to an aged talisman: the Breccbennach (it contained the relics of St. Columba). Bruce roused his men with an inspiring speech that referenced St. Andrew, John the Baptist and Thomas Beckett.

Before the met the English the battle, the Scots held mass on the battlefield. Abbot Maurice of Inchafrrey led the Scots in religious worship, as they all knelt in prayer. Upon witnessing this, Edward II purportedly stated "Yon folk are kneeling to ask mercy." Sir Ingram de Umfraville, a supporter for Balliol who was fighting for the English, translated the essence of the prayer to him: "They ask for mercy, but not from you. They ask God for mercy for their sins. I'll tell you something for a fact, that yon men will win all or die. None will flee for fear of death." Edward II was not intimidated. "So be it," he responded.[202]

Bruce had chosen his battleground wisely: the boggy ground made it difficult for the English cavalry to advance or to launch effective counterattacks. After a brief archery duel, the Scottish schiltrons began advancing rapidly to negate the Welsh longbowmen's deadly advantage in long-range combat. The three formidable formations closed in on the English. Edward Bruce's schiltron attacked the English vanguard, killing Sir Robert Clifford and the Earl of Glouchester. Meanwhile, Randolph's schiltron advanced towards the left flank of the English army. The English archers occasionally found an effective position to open fire on the Scots, but the Scottish cavalry soon charged at them and forced them to retreat from the field. Some of them were even counter-effective; their arrows landed onto the backs of the English army. As the English retreated slowly, the ditches that Bruce's men had dug turned into traps for many English knights. Once they fell in, the English knights and their horses were unable to escape.

A life-or-death clash between English swords and Scottish spears took place in the heart of the field. The ultimate outcome depended on the outcome of this intense hand-to-hand combat. Bruce and his schiltron advanced into this crucial melee, bringing the Gaelic warriors from the Highlands and Islands into the fray. Their presence slowly and surely tipped the scales. As the English began to fall back, the Scots yelled "On them! On them! They fail!"

As the English were driven back by a final and forceful push from the Scottish soldiers and dissolved into a disorganized mess, Edward II was reluctantly escorted away. As the royal standard fled from the battlefield, the English soldiers began to panic. The Scottish schiltrons advanced on the disarrayed English army, slaughtering the English as they attempted to escape. Hundreds of English men and horses drowned in the burn as they made a desperate bid to escape from the merciless Scots.

Edward II himself made a narrow escape to Dunbar, where he made a safe exit to England via ship. Sir James "the Black" Douglas had pursued Edward II and his royal guard of 500 knights all the way to Dunbar. If he had been captured, this would have forced the English to instantly grant Bruce all of his demands. Edward II was lucky, but many of his men were doomed. By the time the battle of ended, thousands of footmen lay dead. A hundred knights and one earl had fallen. The Earl of Pembroke and his Welsh infantry retreated successful to Carlisle, but the Earl of Hereford and several other knights were pursued and captured as they fled southwards. (The Scots reported – perhaps inaccurately – that they had only lost two knights and a few hundred infantrymen).

Without Edward II's capture or death, the English could still continue their war against Bruce. The Scots had nevertheless emerged with *the* major victory against the English during the Middle Ages. Bruce and his commanders had also earned a place in military history. The Battle of Bannockburn[203] and the Battle of the Golden Spurs[204] in 1302 was eventually credited with the introduction of a new form of European warfare, where the infantry were the critical players on the battlefield (instead of the cavalry). With Stirling Castle under his control, Bruce had now acquired complete military control of Scotland. He could now direct his attention towards northern England. (Wallace had been in a similarly enviable position after the Battle at Stirling Bridge).

Bruce also had more personal victories to look forward to. Now that he had consolidated his kingship, Balliol's stalwart supporters were finally motivated to switch allegiances. To obtain the freedom of the English noblemen that had been captured, Edward II was forced to release a few highly significant political prisoners: Bruce's wife Elizabeth de Burgh, his daughter Marjorie, and the Bishop of Wishart. Meanwhile, the Scottish soldiers claimed all the wealth, weapons and provisions that the English had been forced to leave behind.

Chapter 8 – A Worthy King

Bruce's military accomplishments may have rivaled – and even eclipsed – Wallace's after the Battle of Bannockburn, but he still had much insecurity about his reputation. Bruce intended to not only claim the throne of Scotland through sheer military prowess, but also in symbolic terms. His sacrilegious murder of John Comyn needed to be presented as the rightful slaughter of a despicable traitor. He also wanted to advance the case that it was the Bruces, and not John Balliol, who were the rightful heir of the Scottish throne. Any interpretation of his actions as those of an ambitious opportunist needed to be subdued.

There was no question of Bruce's ability to defend Scotland against further English invasions after the Battle of Bannockburn. Between 1315 and 1320, Bruce defeated all the attempts that Edward II could muster. Each invasion ended in a humiliating defeat and a hefty increase to the amount of English funds channeled towards the idea of a Scottish conquest. Between 1315 and 1318, Bruce led his commanders to successfully raid the towns and villages of northern England every year.

Bruce's attempts to attack England from a second front in Ireland in 1315 ultimately proved to be far less successful. His intentions were to force the English to divide their military resources between Ireland and Scotland. Bruce attempted to justify his invasion of Ireland – which was led by his brother Edward – as a righteous endeavor that would free the Irish from English rule. His propaganda campaign for the Irish Wars involved a shared vision of a pan-Gaelic alliance and an emphasis of Scotland and Ireland's shared national ancestry.

Modern historians have pithily described Bruce's campaign for Ireland as "Scotland's Vietnam." After Edward Bruce staged a 300-ship invasion of Ulster, he was crowned as the High King of Ireland in 1316. Historians have suggested that Bruce may have wanted his ambitious brother in this position so that he would not usurp his position. There is also the strategic power of gaining control of the seaboard route to Carlisle.

Some Irish leaders were supportive of this diplomatic logic and ready to reunite with Scotland against their common foe. On the other hand, many Irish people saw little difference between the English and Scottish invasion. The Irish campaign was initially successful. By 1316, Edward Bruce was in a position to gain control of Dublin. Instead, he ordered his troops towards Limerick, where they faced acute problems in receiving their supplies. Edward Bruce was ultimately killed during an ill-conceived assault on antagonistic Irish nobles at the Battle of Faughart in October 1318.[205]

His body was reportedly hacked into four pieces and dispersed to all four corners of Ireland as a warning to the Scots. His head was preserved in salt in a casket and shipped to his brother. Bruce was forced to retire his lofty vision of a "Pan-Gaelic Greater Scotia" and blamed the failure of his endeavors in Ireland on his brother.

In 1318, Bruce reached a high point in his efforts to force Edward II to accept Scotland's independence by re-capturing Berwick. After Bannockburn, the English leaders lacked the unity needed to successfully quell Scotland's thirst for freedom. When Edward II returned to his court, he was forced into a subservient position by his cousin Thomas of Lancaster. Lancaster capitalized on Edward II's military failures to turn himself into the most powerful man in England by 1315. In the end, however, he was not the competent leader that the English desperately needed during this trying period. Within three years, a group of moderate barons led by Aymer de Valence had to serve as arbitrators between Edward II and Lancaster. Once again, the costly infighting could be traced to Edward II's royal favorite(s). Hugh le Despenser and his son had ingratiated themselves into the king's affections. History repeated itself in more ways than one when Lancaster banished both Despensers (after Edward ill-advisedly supported the Despenser son's ambitions to acquire land titles in Wales).

Given these conditions, it is not surprising that Edward II was unable to reclaim Berwick when he besieged it in 1319. Led by Thomas Randolph[206] and James Douglas,[207] the Scottish army was launching disastrous raids on Yorkshire at the same time. This forced him to retreat. In time, however, Edward II did manage to triumph over his baronial nemesis. Lancaster was defeated and captured at Boroughbridge, Yorkshire, in March 1322 and was summarily executed.

In the end, Bruce arrived at the conclusion that he would not be able to secure Scotland's independence on the battlefield. The formidable guerrilla leader turned towards diplomacy instead by reversing his excommunication from the Roman Catholic Church. With the help of Scotland's clergy, he wrote and sent a letter to Pope John XXII in 1320.[208] The Declaration of Arbroath was a historic document that (1) outlined the reasons for why Scotland should remain an independent kingdom; (2) made attempts to rationalize Bruce's previous actions, and; (3) demonstrated that Bruce had unanimous support from the Scottish nobility. Its mission statement is encapsulated in these bold statements: "Never will we on any conditions be subjected to the lordship of the English. It is in truth not for glory, nor riches, nor honours that we are fighting, but for freedom—for that alone, which no honest man gives up save with life itself." There were actually two more letters that were sent to the Pope from Scotland (all with the same intention of securing Scotland's independence). One was sent by the clergy, and one more from the nobles. The letter sent by the nobles was preserved; the other two were lost to time.

Pope John XXII eventually lifted Bruce's excommunication in October 1328. It was ultimately Edward's hopelessly incompetent leadership, however, that finally allowed Bruce to end the First Scottish War of Independence. By 1325, Edward II's favoritism for the Despensers had alienated another powerful figure in his court: his wife Isabella, queen of England. Like Gaveston, the Despensers had earned the wrath of the barons for quickly becoming inseparable from Edward II and accumulating enormous wealth in the process. Like Gaveston, their insatiable greed was compounded by intolerance and arrogance.

Like many barons, Isabella was discontent with how her husband was treating the English nobility. She herself was disenchanted by how her own English estates had been confiscated by the Despensers. Isabella had attempted to broker peace between her husband and the barons before and after Gaveston's murder in 1312; the Despensers were the final straw. In 1325, Isabella sailed home to France on a diplomatic mission. She successfully intervened in a dispute between her brother, Charles IV of France, [209] and Edward II over the latter's land possessions in France (Guyenne, Ponthieu, and Gascony). The lands were secured for England, provided that Edward paid homage to Charles.

While to Paris, Isabella became the mistress of Roger Mortimer and announced that she would not return to England until the Despensers were removed from court.[210] Mortimer was an English baron who had been exiled for his opposition to the Despensers. In September the following year, Isabella and Mortimer invaded England, ordered for the Despensers to be executed, and deposed Edward. Isabella crowned their son Edward III[211] in his place in the first month of 1327. Meanwhile, Edward II was imprisoned until his (possibly violent) death in September that year. (There has nevertheless been recent historical evidence to suggest that his death in 1327 was staged – and that he possibly survived until 1330).

As a young boy, Edward III was in a highly precarious position as the new King of England. Bruce took full advantage of the newly crowned king's vulnerable position by commanding his troops to invade England. Pressured by the unwanted prospect of fighting off the Scottish army and the possibility of a civil war with the rebellious

English nobles, Isabella and Mortimer offered Bruce a truce. In 1328, they signed the hard-won Treaty of Edinburgh-Northampton.

[212] After years of fighting, Bruce had achieved everything he had dreamed of. The truce dictated that (1) Edward III renounced all claims to overlordship over the kingdom of Scotland; (2) peace between England and Scotland would be brokered by an arranged marriage between Bruce's son David and Edward III's sister Joan, and; (3) England officially recognized Scotland's independence and Bruce's rightful position as the King of Scots.

Chapter 9 – Where Your Heart Is

Bruce's son David was only four years old when he was betrothed to Joan. His birth in 1324 had been crucial for Scotland's peace and prosperity. (If Bruce had died without an heir, another costly battle for succession would have been disastrous). By the time Bruce achieved Scotland's independence, he was old and in poor health. Apart from all of his exertions on the battlefield, he had been suffering from an undiagnosed disease – most probably leprosy – for a long time. A year after he signed the Treaty of Edinburgh-Northampton with Isabella and Mortimer, Robert Bruce died at Cardross, Dumbartonshire.

The Scotland he left behind was in a fairly stable state, earning Bruce the moniker "Good King Robert." In 1314, his parliament had decreed that all Scottish nobles who were still allied to England had to forfeit their lands. The forfeited lands were then re-granted to Bruce's supporters through several charters. This allowed some of Bruce's key supporters such as Sir James Douglas, who was knighted for his contributions to the Battle of Bannockburn, to rise to prominence. Douglas was rewarded with large swaths of land in the Selkirk and Roxburgh counties, which would cement the Douglas family's power in the region for years. Bruce had also successfully resurrected the Scottish administration, which had been mostly dysfunctional since 1296. When he died, the system of exchequer audits was functioning once again.

Bruce's dying wish was also fulfilled. His body was buried at Dunfermline Abbey, the traditional final resting place for Scottish kings. On his deathbed, Bruce had instructed his knights to take his heart on a crusade (he had made a vow to participate in a crusade, which remained unfulfilled due to his poor health). Sir James Douglas and his knights obeyed his orders and took it on a crusade in Spain. Douglas was killed during a battle with the Moors, but Bruce's heart was recovered and brought back to Scotland to be buried in Bruce's location of choice: Melrose Abbey. Like Wallace,

Bruce's legendary exploits would live on to touch the hearts and souls of new generations of Scottish people through the form of an epic poem. John Barbour[213] would immortalize his contributions in the 14th-century poem *The Bruce* – the first major work of Scottish literature. Barbour strived for historical accuracy in his art, and went so far as to interview the men who had fought at the Battle of Bannockburn to capture the realities of Bruce's military victory.

In 1921, archeologists discovered a cone-shaped casket that contained a heart while excavating Melrose Abbey.[214] There is no definitive evidence that this particular casket belonged to Bruce, however, since heart burial was a common practice among Scottish royals and aristocrats. The casket and the mummified heart were placed in a lead container and reburied – and then uncovered by another group of archeologists 75 years later.

After being held in Edinburgh for safekeeping for two years, it was reburied in Melrose Abbey (a marker stone commemorates the exact spot). Donald Dewar, Secretary of State for Scotland, observed that the uncertainty of the heart's origins only added to the romance: "There is a strong and proper presumption that this is the heart. But in a sense it does not matter. The casket and the heart are symbols of the man." The simple Scottish sandstone marker over Bruce's final resting place bears a heart, a saltire, and an inscription from *The Bruce*: "A noble hart may have nane ease. Gif freedom failye" (A noble heart cannot be at peace if freedom is lacking).

Chapter 10 – The Son of the Bruce & the Second War for Independence

After the Treaty of Edinburgh-Northampton in 1328, Scotland began the 1330s in a fairly good position. Almost three decades of civil war and war with England had severely sapped the country's resources and morale. However, Robert de Bruce had, for the time being, secured a peaceful end to the English coveting of Scotland. Bruce's death on the 7th of June 1329 left behind a four-year-old son; David II.

David II was crowned king of Scotland on 24 November 1329 [lxxvi], and a guardianship was assumed by Thomas Randolph, who was then Earl of Moray.

In England, Edward III was determined to avenge the humiliation of England by the Scots. Despite having signed the treaty of Edinburgh-Northampton, Edward III was not the same man as his father. And, though he was young, he had a similarly ambitious nature to that of his grandfather, Edward I. Edward had not acted under his own initiative, having instead been pressured by Roger Mortimer, his regent, as well as his mother, Isabella of France.

The "Peace of Northampton," dubbed by the English as "The shameful peace" had failed to account for reparations to a group of nobles who held land and estates in both England and Scotland. Their properties and titles had been given to Bruce's allies, an act that still sat sourly with both the English nobility and Edward III.

England was suffering from a depleted treasury following the wars waged against Scotland, yet the outraged English people and its king were in no position to attempt any further action against Scotland by themselves.

In 1330, the year following the coronation of David II, saw two events occur which would prove to be significant for both Edward and the future of Scotland. Edward III had his regent; Roger Mortimer, executed, thus taking full control of his crown and country.

Secondly, Edward Balliol made an appeal to the now unbridled English king.

The previous king of Scotland, Jon Balliol, who after the English invasion of Scotland in 1296 had been forced to abdicate his throne, had left behind a son; Edward Balliol. Edward Balliol approached the king of England, wanting the return of ancestral lands that he claimed were rightfully his. Before the end of the year, Edward III sent demands to young King David's regent, Thomas Randolph. Randolph delayed responding, despite Edward III pressing the matter with a second request on 22 April 1332. Meanwhile, Balliol and his followers began to prepare for an invasion of Scotland.

The Battle of Dupplin Moor was to be the opening skirmish in what would become known as the Second War of Scottish Independence. The battle was a significant opener to the war, one which was won by Edward Balliol and commander Henry de Beaumont. To circumvent the terms of the Treaty of Northampton, the Scottish rebels and their English allies sailed from several ports in Yorkshire to the Kinghorn in Fife on the 31st of July 1332. [lxxvii] The terms of the Treaty did not permit English forces to cross the Tweed.

From Kinghorn, they eventually marched to Perth. On the 10th of August, the army was camped at Forteviot, a few miles short of the much stronger force led by Donald the Earl of Mar, which was positioned on the heights of Dupplin Moor. A second Scottish force led by Patrick, Earl of Dunbar, was fast approaching Balliol's army from the rear. The predicament lent no courage to the smaller army, and morale in Balliol's camp began to shrink.

Henry Beaumont, the commander of Balliol's army, was accused by the other disinherited lords, claiming he had betrayed them through false promises of Scottish support for Balliol once they had entered Scotland. Beaumont, by far the most experienced soldier on either side, reacted with cool precision, ordering his troops to risk crossing the River Earn at night and launching a surprise attack on the enemy before they could link with the approaching second force.

Overconfident of his superior force, Donald, the Earl of Mar, ordered his army to settle down on the night of 10 August, not bothering to set a watch. At midnight, under the cover of darkness and with no guard present from the opposing army to raise the alarm, Beaumont moved Balliol's force across the Earn to take up a defensive position on high ground at the head of a narrow valley, outflanking Mar.

With the rapid approach of the main Scottish force, Beaumont knew that the time to act was now. The army formed a line, with archers on each flank and men-at-arms at the center, resembling a quarter moon. The Scots, angry that their enemy had outmaneuvered them, charged at the defensively formed English army in disorganized schiltrons, all formation lost to the reckless charge. Mar's wild charge was met with a hail of arrows, falling on the Scottish flanks. The unarmored Scottish footmen, with unvisored helmets, were ill-prepared for the volleys of arrows which fell murderously, thinning their ranks in heartbeats. The superior force, however, was able to get through the storm of arrows and meet the center of the English force, where Beaumont's men-at-arms finally gave some ground. But the unrelenting barrage of arrows thinned out the charging army's flanks, forcing them to push into the middle to escape the rain of death. The larger force lost all ability to maneuver, and the crowded middle ranks of the army were pushed onto the waiting spears of the English.

The Scottish dead were piled high as the battle ended with the English surrounding the mass of bodies. The Scots' losses were heavy; Mar himself was killed as were several other key members of the Scottish army. Estimates of between two and thirteen thousand Scottish dead against relatively light English losses had marked the

first battle of the Second War for Scottish Independence, [lxxvii] and not since the battle of Falkirk had the Scottish felt such a terrible defeat. The worst casualty of all was the loss of national confidence that had grown through the successive victories of King Robert Bruce.

Dunbar's army was still in the field, of a similar number to Mar's prior to his defeat. However, the confidence of Balliol and Beaumont's troops soared. The decimation of Mar's troops was felt through the arriving army; Dunbar was reluctant to engage the force that had so thoroughly dispatched one of equal size to his. The English would learn from this battle most keenly, and the formation adopted by Balliol and Beaumont would become a standard battle order, one which would provide England with many future victories.

The decisive victory granted valuable time to Edward Balliol's invasion, also leaving him well-placed in Scotland to gather supporters and swell his ranks. Balliol saw particularly strong support from the residents of Fife and Strathearn. Not long after his victory at Dunbar, Balliol was crowned the King of Scots, a title he used to gain further support as his army marched across the country, eventually settling in Roxburgh.

While at Roxburgh, with his forces swelling due to the spreading news of his victory against the "usurpers" and claim to the throne, Balliol offered his loyalty to Edward III, pledging to support all of Edward's future battles as well as offering to wed David II's sister, a move that would further legitimize his claim to the throne and expand his lands and fortunes. Balliol then left Roxburgh, moving on to Annan, which would be the site of the Camisade of Annan, a battle between the supporters of Balliol and the loyalist troops of David II, led by Sir Archibald Douglas and John Randolph, 3rd Earl of Moray. Balliol would lose this battle to the Bruce Loyalists but manage to escape, fleeing Scotland to return to Edward in England.

lxxvi

Meanwhile, David II's own resistance had been thrown into turmoil at the death of Thomas Randolph, his regent. Thomas had been a constant companion to Robert de Bruce in his final years and taken over management of the Bruce's household. Robert had decreed before his death that Randolph would serve as David's regent, a role he performed wisely and with honor before his unfortunate death at

Musselburgh. Randolph had been on his way to engage Edward Balliol and his supporters when he died, many believed it to be the result of English poison, but the most likely culprit was a kidney stone.

Edward III invades

Once he had returned to England, Edward Balliol once again offered his loyalty and homage to Edward III, requesting his aid in the combined campaign against Scotland.

Balliol returned to Scotland in March 1333 to lay siege to Berwick-upon-Tweed. Berwick-upon-Tweed held a strategic position on the border between Scotland and England, being the main route for both invasion and trade. The town had a tumultuous past, having been sacked by Edward I in 1296, one of the first actions which marked the beginning of the first Scottish War of Independence. Edward III's justification of the military actions against Berwick-upon-Tweed and the violation of the Treaty of Northampton were due to his claims that Scotland was preparing for war, his incursion being a response to threats from the north.

Balliol crossed the border first with his disinherited Scottish lords on 10 March, accompanied by some English magnates. Edward had invested heavily in the nobles accompanying the campaign, providing grants of over £1,000 to the Englishmen and a similar amount to Balliol and his Scottish nobles. Balliol's army reached Berwick in late March and immediately made moves to encircle the town and cutting off all aid by land, Edward's navy having already done the same by sea.

Edward himself arrived at Berwick with the bulk of the English army on the 9th of May, some six weeks after Balliol had arrived and laid siege. Balliol had not been idle, unleashing a scorched earth policy upon the surrounding lands, ensuring that there was little to no sustenance in the region to resupply the town if the opportunity arose. The town's water supply had already been cut, trenches dug, and all communication out of Berwick was made impossible while

Edwards accompanying craftsman began work on the siege engines required to take the town.

A large Scottish army was gathered just north of the border, under the leadership of Sir Archibald Douglas. He concentrated his energy on swelling the ranks of the army rather than utilizing the troops he already had, except for carrying out some minor raiding into Cumberland. Unfortunately, these raids had little effect in drawing the English away from Berwick and instead provided Edward with justification for his military campaign.

By the end of June, with the full support of the English army, its trebuchets and catapults, and also Edward's Navy, Berwick was close to falling. With its garrison exhausted and half the town destroyed, a truce was requested by the defending commander Alexander Seton. Edward agreed to the truce on the condition that Seton surrender by 11 July.

Douglas was now without options, and the army that had gathered north of the border was compelled into action. Douglas had approximately thirteen thousand troops, significantly more than Edward's nine thousand. On the last day of Seton's truce, the army entered England, marching to the port of Tweedmouth. The little port had been destroyed, having been an obstacle for the large Scottish army, who were eager to provide the relief required by the truce set down by Edward.

A few hundred Scottish cavalries were able to navigate their way across the ruins of the old bridge and then force their way to Berwick. In their minds, and in those of the Scottish garrison at Berwick, the terms of the truce had been satisfied. Edward argued that the relief was to have come from Scotland, or rather the direction of Scotland, while the few hundred Scottish cavalries had entered Berwick from the English side. After much arguing, a fresh truce was agreed to on the provision of relief before the 20th of July. Douglas knew that a foray against Edward in his current defensive position would be disastrous, even with his superior numbers. To draw the English army out to more favorable terrain, Douglas marched the Scottish army south towards Bamburgh, threatening to besiege the town where Edwards's queen was currently in residence. However, Edward was confident in Bamburgh's defenses, and the Scots had not the time to construct the type of machinery needed to breach the fortress. Instead, the Scottish army ravaged the countryside. Edward ignored this, positioning his army on Halidon Hill, a highly defensive position on a rise of some six hundred feet.

Douglas, out of options, had little choice but to engage Edward on the grounds of his choosing. To engage the English army, the Scots descended downhill to the marshy ground that covered the area before Halidon Hill. Once over the marshy ground they still had the hill to climb before reaching the English forces. The journey left the Scottish spearmen vulnerable to English arrows for a long period of time without cover. Casualties were heavy, however the survivors made it to the crest of the hill, climbing towards the waiting spears of the English. The Scottish army broke; their casualties were in the thousands including Douglas himself. Edwards's casualties were numbered at just fourteen.

The next day Berwick's truce expired, and the town surrendered to Edwards's terms.

The loss of Douglas and the troops at Halidon Hill was a tremendous blow to the supporters of David II. The Scottish king would soon be exiled to France, where he would remain until 1341. Edward Balliol was crowned and quickly fulfilled his promises to Edward. Acknowledging fealty and subjection to the Edward, Balliol surrendered Berwick as an inalienable possession of the English Crown". Following later that year, Balliol also yielded Roxburgh,

Edinburgh, Peebles, Dumfries, Linlithgow, and Haddington, [lxxvi] and though Edward did not remove Scottish laws, he did replace the men in charge with his own.

While David II was removed and Edward III attended to the issues of his own kingdom, Balliol was troubled by unrest among both the Scottish nationalists and his own allies. [lxxvi] While Balliol's allies seemed to be deserting him, his enemies were only growing in number. He retired to Berwick, managing to convince Edward III that the situation was under control, though in the meantime more and more of his men were defecting to join those loyal to David II. [lxxvii]

French and English relations were already tense, with Philip VI of France offering shelter to David II. A mutual defensive pact had been signed between Scotland and France in 1295, under the then king Jon Balliol, Edward Balliol's father. After a plea for aid from David's new co-regents, Philip sent an ambassador to England to discuss the recent events between Scotland and England. Unfortunately, not much would be gained by the ambassadors, who; failing to make headway with the disorganized members of David II's loyalist supporters, only succeeded in unwittingly allowing England time to recover their finances. [lxxviii]

In March 1335, having lost confidence in Balliol's ability to hold sway over the Scottish noblemen, Edward began mustering his forces. Scotland was aware of the growing mobilization of English forces and began to quietly prepare. Edward raised his largest army to date, numbering thirteen thousand men, his strategy a three-pronged invasion of Scotland. Balliol would take troops west from Berwick while Edward led his troops north from Carlisle, and a naval force near the Clyde would form the third front of the invasion. The armies encountered little resistance, meeting up at Glasgow and eventually settling in the area of Perth.

In France, an army of six thousand soldiers was openly assembled to aid the Scottish troops. Edward was informed that these troops would be deployed if he did not submit to arbitration by France and the Pope. Edward refused.

Meanwhile, Scottish loyalist forces were not faring well. Andrew Murray agreed to a truce with Edward, lasting from October until Christmas. However, Balliol and his followers were not included in the terms. Balliol, through the support of David III Strathbogie, lay siege against Kildrummy Castle. Murray sent troops after him, routing his force and killing Strathbogie. Balliol would see many more defeats in the coming years that would force him to rely more and more heavily on the English king. [lxxvii]

In May 1336, Edward pushed on with his invasion plans despite the threat from the French. He received reports of the amassing forces of Philip, and intended to block the most likely port of arrival, Aberdeen. Edward moved from Newcastle with a force of four hundred men, swelling his ranks as he marched on Lochindorb, ending Scottish sieges and destroying everything he encountered before burning Aberdeen to the ground.

The English embassy had been attempting to negotiate with Philip VI and David II, however, in August they received final word from Philip; his invasion of England would proceed. French privateers attacked the town of Oxford, also capturing several royal ships. [lxxvi] Edward received word of French actions by September. He abandoned his immediate plans in Scotland and returned to England. However, he was too late to strike back at French ships. He raised funds before returning to Scotland, settling down to winter at the fortress in Clyde after a series of wins and losses. Scotland was under heavy strain, with both English and Scottish forces ravaging the countryside, each trying to eliminate any advantage the other force might acquire. Disease and hunger were rampant among the people.

The Scottish loyalists used the French distractions to their advantage, and by the end of March they had reclaimed most of Scotland north of the Forth and had dealt serious blows to lands owned by Edward Balliol. Edward III was forced to focus on France, vowing to return to Scotland once they had been taken care of. In the meantime, France had also continued to pour supplies into Scotland to aid the Scottish loyalists. The newly provisioned Scottish forces were able to progress further south and into northern England, laying waste to Cumberland and forcing Edward to split his efforts between both French and Scottish threats.

Early winter of 1338 was seen as a turning point for the Scots, and though the ruthless actions of Murray had left such devastation in his own lands that thousands of Scottish people were left without a means to feed themselves, he had effectively ended the possibility for Edward III to establish a stable lordship over southern Scotland. [lxxviii]

Return of the son of the Bruce

David II reached the age of eighteen by the summer of 1341. He returned to Scotland in June of that year, eager to surround himself with his people and begin to establish his own authority. Unfortunately, David made many mistakes, angering some key figures in Scotland's political power base. His authority was undermined by William Douglas, and Robert Stewart swapped the lands they had been given by David. [lxxix]

Skirmishes with the English also continued under David, who conducted several raids into England. In February 1343 the English and French entered into a truce which included Scotland and which was meant to last until September of 1346, through several skirmishes did occur during this time. However, it was not until 1346 that circumstances would change when Philip VI appealed to David II for his support.

Edward II had recently won a dynamic victory in Northern France against Philip at the Battle of Crécy. Philip urged David to invade England to force Edward to return and deal with the northern threat. David mustered a massive force in Perth, but the English had been given enough time to raise a similar force. On 17 October 1346, both armies met near Durham, to engage in what would become known as the Battle of Neville's cross. The battle would be catastrophic for the Scottish forces, with many of their leaders slain and David II himself taken prisoner.

David would remain a prisoner of the English until 1357, with most of his sentence spent in the Tower of London. [lxxix] With many of the Scottish leadership either slain or taken captive, the future was looking bleak. Edward Balliol wasted no time in gathering combatants to him with the intent to launch an excursion back into Scotland. However, despite Balliol's campaign restoring some of the southern Scottish lands back to Edward III, the campaign on a whole made little headway. Edward's attention had been turned back to France.

Over the next few years, Edward would try to use David and his other captive Sir Archibald Douglas to negotiate favorable terms with Scotland. Edward seemed to lose any interest in securing the interests of Balliol, his negotiations requested David hold Scotland as a fief for England, and named Edward III or one of his sons as successors to the Throne should David not produce an heir. [lxxix] The Scottish lords refused. By 1350 Edward had altered his request, instead ransoming David II for a fee of £40,000, the reinstatement of the disinherited lords, and David's agreement to name Edward's son as his successor should he die without children. The Scots seemed to entertain the idea, requesting time for further negotiation. David II himself was permitted to return to Scotland briefly to aid in the negotiations. However, this offer too would fail, and David would return to England.

Years would pass without any agreement between Edward and Scotland. By 1352 parliament convened to decide upon the fate of David, and Scotland did not find the prospect of Scottish submission to the English as a fair trade for the return of their king.

Edward was still heavily involved in the events in France, and in 1354 offered a simple ransom for the return of David, however, the Scots rejected this as well. In 1355, with French backing, Scottish forces launched a successful campaign against Berwick, reclaiming the town. This would prove a mistake, Edward's retaliation was swift and brutal, invading Scotland in an episode that would become known as the Burnt Candlemas; a military campaign focused not on the engagement of enemy forces but simply the destruction of everything within the army's warpath. Edward recaptured Berwick before moving on to sack Haddington. English armies decimated most of Lothian before burning Edinburgh. [lxxvii]

The Second War of Scottish Independence would end with the Treaty of Berwick, one in which Scotland would agree to pay 100,000 merks to England over a ten-year period. [lxxix] Edward Balliol, weary and ill over decades of war and fighting and with little left to show, would rescind his claim for the Scottish throne in exchange for an annuity of £2000. [lxxvi] David II returned to Scotland, to deal with the political discourse and rivalries common in any court at the time.

The Second War of Scottish Independence demonstrated more so than any other event in the previous hundred years the fruitlessness of a struggle between England and Scotland. Despite the many maneuverings and battles of the period, the two countries were left ultimately in a stalemate, with little gain on either side. Scotland retained some semblance of its independence and England retained its reputation as a leading figure in European powers.

Conclusion

Bruce's death wish (to have his heart be taken on a religious crusade) points towards how his life had pivoted from a personal quest for power to a more symbolic pursuit of a grander, loftier, and more ambiguously defined "Scottish cause." The Scottish nobility may have not been consistent in their support for the right of the Scottish realm to maintain its laws and customs without influence and interference from the English, but it was apparent that the desire for the continued existence of the Kingdom of Scotland had always prevent the Scots from simply submitting themselves to Edward I's overlordship.

William Wallace's rise from being an unknown squire to a war leader and a Guardian of Scotland is a potent symbol for how Scottish men from all walks of life were willing to risk everything in opposing English attempts at conquest. It is certainly worth pointing out that England's ambitions to exert authority over its northern neighbor did not end with Edward I, his son, or his grandson. From the 1290s to Henry IV's reign in 1400, each English king led his own costly attempt to subdue the Scots. Each of these attempts eventually failed.

Edward III, despite being himself a skilled leader akin to his grandfather Edward I, learnt better than most the costs involved in an attempt to subdue the Scots. His own life littered with resentment towards the struggles against the Scottish, his ambition to become overlord of Scotland discarded with the Treaty of Berwick.

The phenomenon of Scottish resistance was nevertheless more complex than a simple "us versus them" scenario. Civil war between the Scottish nobles and local warfare in various towns and counties was part of everyday life through the First Scottish War of Independence. The battles that were fought against the absorption of Scotland into England were nevertheless fought in the name of King John Balliol, who was commonly accepted as the rightful ruler of the realm.

Bruce's bid for the throne in 1306, after the murder of John Comyn, was thus a shocking departure from common expectations. His sacrilegious and criminal action prompted the Scottish supporters of John Balliol and Edward I to unite to oppose him. Bruce's challenge was thus twofold from the very beginning. He had to hold his own ground against the English army on the battlefield *and* to rightfully establish himself as the ruler of Scotland. In time, Bruce decisively demonstrated his military competence by emerging victorious at the Battle of Bannockburn.

Military success alone was nevertheless insufficient for Bruce to mount an undisputed claim for royal rights. Bruce needed the symbolic weight afforded by documents like the Declaration of the Clergy in 1309 and the Declaration of Arbroath in 1320 to support his position as the rightful king of the community. Bruce attempted to discredit Balliol's claim to the throne by advancing the argument that a king who submitted to England had forfeited his rights. Bruce's propaganda aimed to establish himself as the rightful defender of the realm who could defend its freedom against the formidable English army.

Given his precarious standing, Bruce was always paranoid about the possibility of being undermined and displaced. The enemies he had exiled – chiefly Edward Balliol[215] – were biding their time, waiting for the right moment to strike. Bruce also had to contend with Scottish nobles and magnates who were fatigued by the constant warfare Scotland had to endure under Bruce's command. Within a few months after the Declaration of Arbroath, Bruce had to contend with the unsuccessful conspiracy of 1320. Its aim was to replace him with Balliol and establish a peaceful truce with England. Bruce was also troubled by his lack of a suitable adult heir that could take his place. To better ensure that the Scottish nobility would support the authority of the Bruce family, he carefully promoted and enhanced the standings of his supporters. The magnates who opposed him found their lands and titles redistributed to Bruce's supporters – who were encouraged to cultivate a personal stake in the survival of the Bruce royal line.

The Treaty of Edinburgh-Northampton initially appeared to achieve everything that Bruce had fought for. The English had withdrawn their claims of overlordship. Scotland was finally at peace, and Bruce finally had a male heir to continue his hard-won royal line. And yet, a mere three years after Bruce's death, Scotland was in turmoil once again. In 1332, Edward Balliol - the son of the king that the majority of Scots had accepted before Bruce's unexpected campaign for the throne – led an invasion of Scotland. He was supported by a group of English nobles whose lands in Scotland had been seized and redistributed by Robert Bruce. Despite their larger numbers, the army led by Donald, Earl of Mar and regent for David II[216] (who was then eight years old) was defeated at Dupplin Moor (near Perth). Edward Balliol was then crowned king at Scone. A new civil war between the Balliol supporters and Bruce supporters had been triggered.

Seeing the opportunity to restore England's might during the reign of his grandfather, Edward III denounced the peace that Isabella and Mortimer had brokered with Robert Bruce in 1328 as being "shameful." Despite being only 14 when he had been heavily persuaded by his mother and Roger Mortimer to sign it, he had been deeply troubled by the treaty. Not long after his marriage to Philippa at York, he established his independence and position as England's ruler. In 1330, he snuck into a Nottingham castle where a council was held and took Mortimer prisoner.

Mortimer was swiftly executed. As Isabella's paramour, Mortimer had thoroughly abused his position as the most powerful man in England. He had acquired the lordships of Denbigh, Oswestry, and Clun for himself, and received additional lordships from the queen. His greed, arrogance, and unpopular policy instigated deep hostility from the barons. Henry of Lancaster thus helped the young king to capture Mortimer, condemn him for his crimes, and hang him as a traitor. His enormous estates were then forfeited to the crown. Edward III respected his mother and forgave her for the illicit liaison, but did not hesitate to end her political influence. Forced into retirement, Isabella eventually joined the Poor Clares, an order of nuns, in her later years.

Edward III took advantage of David II's young age to help the exiled Scottish barons restore Edward Balliol to the Scottish throne. In return, Balliol would recognize Edward III's overlordship and ordered for the cession of southern Southland. This earned Balliol widespread resentment for being a puppet of an English king. On December 1332, a Scottish resistance force led by Sir Archibald Douglas defeated Balliol at Annan, Dumfries. With Edward III's help, Balliol was able to defeat and kill Douglas during a second confrontation at Halidon (on the outskirts of Berwick) in July the following year. He thus cemented an uncertain authority over the majority of Scotland.

David II was forced to flee to France in 1334 to ensure his own safety. He was received warmly by King Philip VI. In 1339 and 1340, he assisted the French king in his unproductive campaigns against Edward III. Like his father, David II eventually returned to regain his authority over Scotland. England's ambition for conquest was thwarted once again. With the help of experienced local captains and guardians, the Bruce faction was able to defeat Balliol's forces and the English garrisons. David II returned to Scotland as King in 1341, in control of a majority of the realm.

Inspired to emulate his father's military accomplishments, David II embarked on a series of ultimately unsuccessful invasions of northern England. His efforts culminated in the ambitious battle at Neville's Cross outside Durham in 1346. His army was defeated and David II himself was captured by the English. If Robert Bruce had been captured by the English during his campaigns, Scotland's quest for independence would have certainly been doomed. By this time, however, Edward III's zeal to establish an overlordship over

Scotland had waned. He did mount a final invasion in 1356, but there was no great effort to subjugate Scotland within the intervening decade. Instead, the conflict between the English and Scottish were confined to small battles over Scottish border communities and control of surviving English strongholds in Scotland. In 1409, only Roxburgh and Berwick remained under English control.

England may have been the wealthier and more powerful nation, but its leaders were unable to convert their military successes into a final and unrelenting victory. Despite winning control of key Scottish strongholds and maintaining the presence of the English army in various Scottish territories, undisputed control of Scotland proved to be highly elusive (particularly in the western and northern regions). There was also the problem of limited resources. Edward I's attempts were most successful because he had the luxury of making the Scottish conquest the sole focus of his attention during the early 1300s and mid-1330s. His successors had to divide their attention between domestic conflicts and continental wars; for example, Edward III's Hundred Years' War with France, which unfolded between 1337 and 1453.[217] (Given France's history of providing refuge to David II and its support for the Scots during Edward III's attempts at conquest, it was natural for David II to (unsuccessfully) invade England in 1346 in return).

By 1356, Edward Balliol had given up hope of reclaiming the Scottish throne for himself. He resigned his titles and relinquished all his lands to Edward III in January that year. He would die without leaving behind any heir, ending the Balliol line's claim to the throne. After being held an English prisoner for a decade, David II was released in 1357 in return for a hefty ransom. In his absence, Robert Stewart (his nephew and heir) and William Douglas had been defending and leading the realm.

David II's attempts to expand his royal power, wealth and influence – despite being burdened by the ransom he owed to England III –

alienated Stewart and Douglas. He also attempted to allow Edward III's son to succeed the Scottish throne in exchange for his impossible ransom to be repaid (he did not have any heir to succeed him). Many found this proposition unthinkable – especially Stewart, who was the rightful successor to the throne. David II and his knights had to quash the rebellion organized by Stewart and Douglas. In the end, the Scottish parliament repudiated the idea of an English succession. In his final years, David II inspired additional political opposition for his financial extravagance.

After his death in early 1371, Robert II[218] assumed the throne of Scotland as the first Stewart sovereign. Being the maternal grandson of Robert Bruce, he had been Scotland's presumptive heir for the majority of his fifty-four years. He aimed to consolidate his wealth and power to ensure that the throne remained with the Stewart lineage. By furthering the mutual interests of his extended family, he was able to engender a climate of political stability in the 1370s. By 1384, however, internal rivalries would disrupt the peace. Robert II was usurped by his own heir and eldest son, John Earl of Carrick. In 1388, Carrick himself was displaced by his own younger brother, Robert of Fife.

These were not simply toxic family rivalries for ultimate power. They were also a reflection of the failure of the monarchy and its lieutenants to maintain the stability of the kingdom's regional communities – a task that had been made considerably more complex by the long years of war with England. The Southern magnates demanded support and assistance in attempts to combat the English. Meanwhile, there were concerns that the magnates of the Highlands were impinging on the rights and interests of their Lowland counterparts. Dissatisfied with the inability of the monarch to protect their interests, Scotland became more dominated by regionalized politics from 1388 onward. The distinction between the king himself and his chief subjects – who might be elevated for the purposes of political or military expedience – had been blurred.

Despite these problems, the Scottish crown remained independent from England until 1603. After the death of Elizabeth I, James VI of Scotland ascended to the English throne and became James I. This marked the first time where England and Scotland were ruled by a single monarch. This tradition would continue until 1707, when the Act of Union was signed. This treaty meant that England and Scotland would be united as Great Britain.[219] It established peace, open borders and prosperity between both lands in a way that William Wallace and Robert Bruce would probably have never imagined. And yet, Scottish culture flourished and retained its own distinct identity. This was partly due to the separation of the court system and the church – a consequence of Wallace and Bruce's long and difficult struggle for an identity to call their own.[220] Their battles and deeds live on in Scotland's national myths, instilling pride in the nation's separate identity and existence. Each generation extolls the battles these national heroes won and lost, in their valiant efforts to ensure the continuity of crown, community of the realm, and nation.

Part 3: William Wallace

A Captivating Guide to a Freedom Fighter and Martyr Who Impacted Scottish History and Scotland's Independence from England

Chapter 1 – Mysterious Origins

The gory conditions of Wallace's death are well documented, but there is insufficient evidence to conclusively settle the case for his origins. His exact year of birth is unknown. Records have been as varied as 1260 and 1278, but 1270 serves as the most probable year. His location of birth has also been contested. Since his name was styled 'of Ellerslie' due to the land that was owned by his father, Sir Malcolm Wallace (who was styled 'of Auchenbothie and Ellerslie'), many assumed that he was born in the Renfrewshire town of Elderslie.[234] The town still proclaims itself to be birthplace of Scotland's national hero. Its attractions include a small castellated house that is deemed to be his birthplace, an old yew tree known as Wallace's Yew, Wallace's Tavern, and a distinctive monument that was erected in 1970.

Much of the confusion about Wallace's origins comes from the epic poem *The Wallace*,[235] written by fifteenth-century court poet Blind Harry (c. 1440 – 1492). Blind Harry claimed to have based his poem on a prose manuscript that was compiled by John Blair. Blair had been Wallace's friend in school, and then his chaplain. This manuscript has never been found (some doubt it ever existed), so there is no way of proving how faithfully or unfaithfully Blind Harry adhered to it. After all, Blind Harry was probably not born blind or as uneducated as he presented himself to be. He probably also drew from the many myths, anecdotes, and folktales about Wallace that circulated during his time. In any case, historians have already located many historical errors in the text.

Historian James Mackay argues that Wallace had actually been born in the lesser-known county of Ayrshire, within the district of Kyle.[236] Ellerslie, or Elderslie, are different variants of the same name, which has been used to refer to Ayrshire and Renfrewshire in maps and documents (Ayrshire is confusingly also known as Elderslie today). Ellerslie, Ayrshire, had been a simple hamlet that revolved around coal mining and brickworks until the Second World War. Little of it remains today.

Where the Wallaces came from is also a matter of debate. The medieval names Walays, Waleys, or Wallensis refer to a Welshman within the English languages spoken by the Englishmen and Scotsmen of the time. It is thus certainly possible that the Wallaces in the area were medieval immigrants from Wales (an origin story that Blind Harry perpetuated). James Mackay, however, notes that the surviving land titles and buildings cannot conclusively connect William Wallace to the more eminent Wallaces that could trace back their ancestral roots to Wales. There are also contradictory speculations that suggest Wallace might have Anglo-Danish ancestry instead.

What historians can agree on, however, is the fact that Wallace was born in Scotland in 1270, when it was wealthy and peaceful. King Alexander III had been ruling since 1249; political stability had ushered in an era of prosperity and harmony. [237] This was a country adorned with majestic cathedrals, magnificent abbeys, and grand monasteries. There were also hundreds of castles that were home to the aristocrats, barons, and knights, and stately homes that belonged to the landed classes. By this time, the Scots had been under the rule of only one monarch for nearly four generations. Many of them were more in touch with royals than a national identity. Much of the economic and political activity of the era revolved around Berwick, which was strategically placed at the mouth of the River Tweed. At its port, Scottish merchants traded with the Low Countries, northern Germany, and Scandinavia. The country's capital, Edinburgh, was similar in size to Berwick. There were nearly half a million people in Scotland at the time, while there were approximately 2 million in England. The relationship between the two countries was peaceful, but their border had never been definitively delineated. As a result, there had been many territorial disputes in the past.

Wallace was born into what would retrospectively be known as Scotland's "golden age." Scottish agriculture surpassed English agriculture during Alexander III's reign, with a dominant wool and cattle industry.[238] With low taxes, the people could enjoy the fruits of their labor by indulging in alcohol and a hearty diet. There were bridges and good roads that could speed up trade via wheeled carts, horseback, and wagons. Scotland was an exporter of fish, timber, wool, and hides. It looked toward northern Europe for international relations, instead of England.

As a young Wallace grew up with few worries, King Henry III of England died. He was replaced by his son, King Edward I, the man who would become his most powerful opponent. Both men's ambitions reflected the prosperity of their respective countries. Edward I was known as "Longshanks" for his tall stature, while Wallace would grow to a staggering height of two meters (six-foot-seven). When you consider the fact that the average height of an adult man at the time was only slightly over five feet, Wallace must have stood out easily after he hit puberty. Blind Harry's poem has been deemed to be accurate when it comes to describing his physicality.[239] Wallace is noted for his large stature, broad shoulders, handsome face, great limbs, sturdy neck, wavy brown hair, piercing eyes, and overtly "manly make."

In an era where close combat (possibly with the help of a sword and dagger) was the order of the day during physical conflicts, Wallace's superhuman stature undeniably served him well. Without exemplary mental attributes, however, it is unlikely that he would have been able to attract and lead his followers toward historic glory. Historians speculate that he received a secular and religious education from the monks in his area, as well as from his parents. Apart from learning to read and write, he would have also been equipped with horse riding and martial skills. He was trained in the art of fighting with the dirk (a long thrusting dagger) and the claymore (a tall two-handed sword). A claymore was nearly six feet in length, taller than most men living at the time. When a figure as tall and strong as Wallace whirled it into an opponent, it was enough to slash through the armor of the time.

Wallace was probably between eleven to thirteen years old when Edward I finished his conquest of Wales (in 1283, after six years). In 1285, he traveled to Paris to pay homage to its new King, Philip the Fair.[240] He would remain there for three years, apparently secure that England and Wales were firmly under control. Instead, many of his ministers and judges turned to greater heights of corruption while he was away. After returning in 1289, he decided to expel all Jews from his kingdom, using them as a scapegoat for the political chaos and economic strife at the time. He then turned his ambitious gaze toward Scotland.

Chapter 2 – Coming of Age in Crisis

When Wallace was approximately fourteen years old, Scotland was struck with a national crisis. On 18 March 1286, King Alexander attended a council in Edinburgh Castle. After that, he enjoyed fine wine with his barons over a good meal as a storm brewed outside. Instead of staying the night at the Castle, he decided to return home to Kinghorn via horseback. Many surmised that he was eager to return home to his young wife, Joleta of Dreux, France, who was half his age. He eventually became separated from his three esquires and two local guides in the darkness and howling winds. When they found him the next day, he was dead. His body was at the rocks at the foot of the cliffs.

The people had been expecting a male heir after the King's recent re-marriage (in 1285; after his first wife, Princess Margaret of England, died in 1275) and were stunned by the news of his death. This tragic news followed the death of Alexander's first two sons in 1281 and 1284. After two weeks of mourning, Alexander's granddaughter, Margaret of Norway,[241] was sworn in as the nation's sovereign lady. Her mother had died in childbirth, leaving her in the care of her father, King Eric II of Norway.[242] A provisional was established, with six Guardians of the Peace elected as regents. The Guardians were comprised of two earls, two barons, and two bishops.

Peace was maintained for the following three years. After that, powerful and competing factions began to appear on the national scene. The throne was empty, and there were powerful political players who aspired to occupy it. During this time, it is possible that Wallace and his father were called up for military service to defend the realm by the Guardians. The revolt was eventually resolved, but the authority of the Guardians had been called into question. As the composition of the Guardians changed with the death of two of the earls (one due to old age, the other murdered by his own family),

Wallace's future was under discussion. As a landless younger son, Wallace was poised to pursue a religious career. His keen intelligence made this a good fit, and the parson of Dunipace – where Wallace was staying with an uncle – was known to be a wealthy and benevolent man. His uncle taught him moral maxims in Latin and exposed him to the eminent classical authors.

Plans were made for Margaret of Norway to marry Lord Edward, the five-year-old son of King Edward I when both were of age. The Treaty of Birgham was signed on 18 July 1920, uniting the two royal individuals while maintaining the separation of Scotland and England.[243] Margaret was to be Scotland's 'true lady, queen and heir,' married to an English prince to preserve the peace between the two countries. Edward, on the other hand, intended to exert control over Scotland through matrimonial rights. When she died due to seasickness during the trip from Norway to Scotland, however, Scotland's hopes for independence were in peril. With her death, an ancient Scottish dynasty had arrived at a tragic end.

There were no less than thirteen candidates for the throne, each claiming a lineage from the Scottish royal family. If Margaret's mother had been alive, then her husband, Eirik II of Norway, would have a rightful claim to the throne. Some of the claims were based on being illegitimate offspring, which could not be granted serious consideration. Two primary candidates emerged from all this contestation: John de Balliol[244] and Robert de Bruce.[245] Since each man was backed by armed forces, Scotland appeared to be on the brink of a civil war.

If England's King Edward had plans to take advantage of Scotland's leadership vacuum, he had to wait until the customary mourning period for his wife's passing was over. James Mackay has noted that Eleanor may have had a positive moral influence on her husband; her death thus freed him from any moral barriers toward violence and tyranny. While agreeing to advise the Scots on their succession crisis, he revealed to his privy council that he had plans to subdue Scotland as he had done with Wales.

Unfortunately for Wales and Scotland, Edward was one of England's most effective kings. The Scots would eventually refer to him as "Scottorum malleus" – the Hammer of the Scots – after he died in 1307. The reign of his father, Henry III,[246] had been fraught with internal instability and military ineptitude. When he assumed the throne in 1272, he successfully negotiated peaceful relations between England's restless barons and united them under his rule. As a young man, he had proven himself on the battlefield as a soldier and military leader.

He was also a well-read monarch with an interest in new ideas that would reform the English government and administration. His means may have been highly unethical, but he was similarly successful when it came to raising money. He used his Parliament to maintain stability and collect large amounts of taxes from the population during his prosperous reign. In 1275, he imposed the popular Statute of Jewry, which imposed exorbitant levels of taxation on England's Jewish population. In 1290, all of England's Jews were expelled without their financial assets and property. He was thus financially well positioned to embark on an ambitious campaign of expansion.

The Guardians of Scotland's decision to invite Edward to adjudicate the competing claims to the Scottish throne eventually proved to be severely counterproductive. After years of fairly peaceful coexistence, they had wrongly assumed that English rule over Scotland was a matter of the past. King Willian I had acknowledged England's King Henry II as Scotland's feudal lord in 1174, but Scotland had retained a great degree of its independence throughout the thirteenth century. As such, they invited Edward – as an influential king and a notable expert on the legal aspects of statecraft – to be the judge on who was the rightful heir to the Scottish throne.

On 10 May 1291, King Edward proclaimed his rule over Scotland in front of an assembly of Scottish nobles and clergy. This justified his position as adjudicator in who was the next ruler of Scotland – and his position as Lord Paramount of Scotland. After the Scottish noblemen objected, he granted them three weeks to formulate a rebuttal. Meanwhile, he began marshaling his army to prepare for a possible military confrontation.

All the competitors for the throne eventually acknowledged Edward as Lord Paramount and consented to accepting his judgment. With most of them were in possession of large estates in England, the failure to do so would have almost certainly resulted in the forfeiture of these assets. Edward was careful enough to ensure that each competitor's acknowledgment was written down and graced with their official seal. After that, he ordered that every Scottish castle be surrendered to him temporarily until a successor had been chosen. Furthermore, all Scottish officials were to be replaced with Englishmen. All Scottish nobility, knights, freemen, and religious leaders were to swear their loyalty to Edward by 27 July or face severe penalties. Wallace's father, Sir Malcolm Wallace, refused to administer the oath and fled north with his eldest son when English officials were upon him.

Wallace was seventeen or eighteen at this time. He was sent to a nearby church school, which trained young men for a lifelong career as a priest. He met John Blair at this school. Blair would become a Benedictine monk and Wallace's comrade in arms, as well as the author of a Latin biography that Blind Harry would use as a reference for his epic poem.[247] There was some resistance in Dundee, but in general, the entire country was not particularly invested in resisting Edward's demands.

In December 1292, John Balliol was crowned King of Scotland:

> As it is admitted that the kingdom of Scotland is indivisible, and, as the king of England must judge of the rights of his subjects according to the laws and usages of the kingdoms over which he

> reigns; and as, by the laws and usages of England and Scotland in the succession to indivisible heritage, the more remote in degree of the first line of descent is preferable to the nearer in degree of the second line; therefore, it is decreed that John Balliol shall have seisin of the kingdom of Scotland.[248]

He arguably had the better claim to the throne than Robert Bruce, being descended from an older royal sister. Bruce had argued that his claim was superior since he was the son of David I's great-granddaughter while John Balliol was the grandson of the great-grand-daughter (i.e. he was one less generation removed from the royal lineage). Balliol also owned land in the north of England, which made him likelier to acquiesce to Edward's mandates. Edward wasted no time in pressuring Balliol to accept his rule over Scotland and begin to assert his powers. When Balliol was crowned, Scotland was effectively under English occupation.

Scottish nobility may have conceded to the new status quo, but the common people did not simply accept the presence of the occupying English forces in their daily lives. They were fiercely proud of their national heritage and despised their elites for cowardly surrendering their authority to the English. Brawls and riots between the English soldiers and Scottish villagers and townspeople began to occur sporadically. One of these conflicts would claim the life of Sir Malcolm Wallace, leaving his son with a lifelong bitter resentment toward the English invaders.

Chapter 3 – Defiance and Compliance

Given the lack of concrete evidence, historians are unsure of the precise details of Wallace's evolution into a formidable guerrilla leader. According to Blind Harry, Wallace began to brazenly defy Edward's rule not long after his father's death. It thus appears that he began to take decisive actions to avenge his father and alleviate the oppression of his countrymen in 1291. The castle of Dundee, which had fallen under the possession of an English baron, served as the first stage for his defiance.

The baron, Brian Fitz-Alan of Bedale, was also a Guardian and Justice of Scotland. The castle was under the care of Selby, a constable that had inflicted much harm to the local community. His twenty-year-old son was known for causing mischief in the town on a daily basis with his friends. That December, the young Selby spotted Wallace's enormous frame and bright green clothes in the street. When Selby confronted him, he made fun of Wallace's appearance: "Thou Scot, abide; what devil clothed thee in so gay a garment? An Irish mantle were the right apparel for thy kind; a Scottish knife under thy belt to carry; rough shoes upon thy boorish feet."[249] He then demanded that Wallace surrender the dirk at his belt. Wallace responded by using it to stab him in the heart.

The crowd's interference allowed Wallace to wound Selby's comrades and make a quick exit. On his way to his uncle's townhouse, he met his uncle's housekeeper. After she learned of what he had done, he quickly had him wear one of her gowns and sat him down at her spindle. When the English soldiers arrived, they were fooled by the disguise. After failing to locate Wallace, they threatened to burn down the town unless the villagers surrendered him. Under the cover of night, Wallace escaped to Kilspindie via the alleys and back courts.

When the Dundee governor summoned all Scottish residents to appear at a court of enquiry, Wallace decided to leave the area. He disguised himself once again, this time as a pilgrim. He kept a short sword hidden under his gown. They pretended to be headed toward the shrine of Saint Margaret at Dunfermline (an English-born saint who had initiated the Anglicization of Scotland) whenever they were questioned by English patrolmen. By the time they arrived at Ellerslie, Wallace had been outlawed for murdering young Selby. His mother remained there while he headed to Reccarton to live with his uncle, Sir Richard Wallace.

On 23rd of February 1292, Wallace went on a fishing excursion with a servant, but without his weapons. There, five English soldiers demanded that he surrender his catch to them. Wallace decided to offer them half; the group's leader dismounted from his horse and seized the entirety of his catch. Wallace's refusal to submit eventually prompted the soldier to attack him with his sword. Wallace used his fishing-pole to defend himself and struck his opponent across the cheek. The blow was powerful enough to knock him off his feet and send his sword soaring through the air. Wallace seized the sword and killed his opponent by aiming at his neck. When the other four soldiers attacked, Wallace sliced through one of them to his collarbone and sliced off another's arm. The other two fled, leaving Wallace to finish off the one-armed soldier. Wallace took the soldier's gear and horses, and then escaped with his young page into the safety of the forest. The story of Wallace's exploits at Irvine Water would survive to be his one of his earliest episodes of heroism.

While Wallace hid himself in the countryside, King John was negotiating the extent to which he could bring himself to oppose King Edward. Edward had warned that he would interfere in the country's affairs should John fail to "do justice" to his subjects and was likely indignant of the fact that he had to repeat his homage to Edward multiple times. In 1292, Edward flexed his influence by deciding a case at Newcastle. Roger Bartholomew had appealed to a higher authority after claiming that the Guardians of Scotland had treated him unfairly when presiding over his complex triple lawsuit. King John argued that Edward was violating the Treaty of Birgham, which mandated that all Scottish lawsuits be determined in Scotland. In response, Edward pronounced that he had the right to judge each and every Scottish case that was presented to him. He then coerced King John to acknowledge that the Treaty of Birgham was now void, and his actions were legally valid. Such maneuvers placed King John with little options but to comply, as the Scottish nobility – which had nurtured close ties with England for over two generations – were generally unwilling to support him in protest. This case established a precedent of appealing to the English courts when the Scottish courts made an unfavorable decision.

Edward maintained a position that he was only undermining King John's authority for the sake for maintaining law and order in Scotland, but it was clear to most observers that he was consciously undermining King John's position. This struggle for power swiftly eroded the relationship between the two leaders. In October 1293, Edward suffered the very same humiliations he had inflicted on King John. King Philip of France was his own feudal superior, and he decided to halt all trade between his country and England after a few English sailors went on a rampage at the La Rochelle port.

In response, Edward declared war against France in October 1294. Philip got Adolf of Germany to remain on neutral terms and secured the alliance of Florence of Holland and Eirik II of Norway; Edward was already dealing with a rebellion in Wales and needed all the assistance he could get. He thus ordered King John to marshal his forces and report to London by 1 September 1294. John seized the opportunity to rebel. On 22 October, he openly defied Edward by allying Scotland with Norway and France.

Edward prepared his armed forces and ships to prepare for a northern confrontation. He ordered King John to relinquish ownership of the castles and burghs of Berwick, Jedburgh, and Roxburgh and ordered English sheriffs to seize all of King John's assets in England. The first real confrontation between the Scots and English took place at the English town of Carlisle. Unable to penetrate its defenses, the Scots burned down the cottages and dwellings of its poorest denizens, which were outside its walls. They then pillaged, burned, and looted the villages, monasteries, and churches in the countryside before retreating past the Scottish border.

The English army – which then was comprised of three thousand foot soldiers and five thousand horsemen – retaliated by attacking Berwick, Scotland's largest city at the time. A few English merchants had been murdered at the port there five weeks earlier by a mob, which had then proceeded to loot their warehouses. Edward apparently intended to turn Berwick into an example. The townspeople were initially successful in defeating four of the five English ships that descended upon them. After that, however, they were in for a massacre. The town was ill-prepared for a military onslaught, but a local Flemish archer was successful in shooting down Richard of Cornwall, Edward's cousin. Edward ordered for the archer's base, the Red Hall, to be burned down to the ground. Over three days, thousands of townsmen, women, and children were raped and killed without mercy. Edward only ordered for his men to stop after witnessing a townswoman giving birth while one of his rampaging soldiers hacked her body to bits. By the time he called off the slaughter, between seventeen and twenty thousand Scottish townsfolk had died, nearly the entire population of Berwick at the time.

Edward had intended for the massacre to terrorize the entire population of Scotland. After generations of peaceful relations between the two countries, this bloody episode was intended to secure his authority over the country. Scottish historian and economist John Hill Burton noted that he had underestimated the common people's immense pride and honor, as well as their willingness to risk their lives in battle to defend it: "In his Norman sublimity, seeing only the persons worth seeing, the nobles, scarcely a step below himself in dignity and pretension, and of his own race, he had reckoned without that hitherto silent and inarticulate entity, the Scottish people."[250]

Instead of admitting defeat, the Scottish people united to support their king's defiance. On 5 April, King John formally renounced his allegiance to the English throne. Scottish bands attacked Redesdale, Tynedale, Cockermouth, and Hexham to avenge the atrocities at Berwick. Meanwhile, Edward set to work at rebuilding the very town that he had so thoroughly destroyed. After reinforcing its defenses, he designated Berwick as the administrative center of his new Scottish government in September 1296. Satisfied and smug with the knowledge that the Scottish elites would not unequivocally rally behind a king many perceived to be weak and ineffectual, he began planning his second attack.

He sent the English army northward, leading to confrontations with the Scottish army at Buchan. With his experienced horsemen, superior numbers, and veteran leaders, his army was able to secure a quick victory. 130 important Scottish knights were taken prisoner alongside several earls and influential magnates. After this, the spirit of Scottish resistance plummeted. The great Scottish castles – Roxburgh Castle, Edinburgh Castle, and Stirling Castle – were either conquered or abandoned. On July 2, King John formally surrendered his kingdom to England, while stating that his alliance with France was a mistake. Edward responded by subjecting him to ceremonial humiliations. Edward had the royal insignia ripped from John Balliol's surcoat, leaving him with the nickname Toom Tabard (empty coat) from then on. He was then shipped to England and placed under a comfortable house arrest.

With its king out of the way, Edward proceeded to further erode Scotland's national identity. He removed the Stone of Destiny (*Lia Fail*), the legendary basalt stone where every Celtic Scottish king had been crowned. It had been in the country since the sixth century after allegedly being brought over from the Holy Land under the care of Scota, the Pharaoh of Egypt's daughter, who lent the country her name. Edward arranged to have himself crowned on the stone, and then sent it to Westminster Abbey along with Scotland's crown jewels, which were only returned in 1996. Edward also shipped away three chests filled with royal records and other important archives. Whether they were lost, hidden, or destroyed, these precious documents were never recovered.

On 28 August 1296, Edward held his parliament at Berwick. The agenda was for the country's prominent bishops, earls, barons, abbots, and priors to pay homage to him and pledge their loyalties. He appointed a guardian of the land, a treasurer, and a chancellor. Edward did not establish himself as the King of Scotland; everyone paid homage to him as the King of England, Lord of Ireland, and Duke of Guyenne. Robert Bruce, Lord of Annandale, who had been allied with Edward throughout King John's rule, had been expecting to be named as John's successor. Edward was not interested in establishing another figurehead. When Bruce made his intentions known, Edward retorted with, "Have we nothing else to do but win you kingdoms?" [251] Edward left the country eleven days after the ceremony, with the intention of focusing on his relations with France and other important matters. When winter came, a majority of the English soldiers there made the trip home. A few garrisons remained in all of Scotland's castles.

Chapter 4 – The Prophecy

Apart from the incident at Irvine Water, little concrete information about William Wallace's life during King John's rule is known. We know, however, that he came of age at a time when Scottish independence was a mirage. Everyone was more or less aware that their king had limited authority and influence over the matters in his own country. Important Scottish fortresses were in the hands of the English. English soldiers roamed the countryside, ready to exert their might against any common people who dared to depart from the expected humility and subservience. The usual processes of law and order were being eroded.

Naturally, William Wallace's exploits as an outlaw in the countryside throughout these years are not well documented. The myth that prevails is one that is similar to the legend of Robin Hood's brand of vigilante justice in the forests of Nottingham. Blind Harry describes him as a heroic defender of a fallen people; an embodiment of the people's desire to tip the scales of power in their favor:

> Although only eighteen years of age, he was seemly, robust and bold. He carried for weapons either a good sword or knife and with such he often had encounters with their English foes. When he found one without his fellow, such a one did no further harm to any Scot. To cut his throat or to stab him suddenly he did not miss. Nor could anyone trace how he came by his death.[252]

Wallace's indiscriminate savagery against the English may seem questionable and barbaric by today's standards, but they make sense when one considers the brutalities of the era. In the 1290s, the mortality rate was exceptionally high. Scottish people were routinely punished for various minor offences by flogging, mutilation, and public hanging. Without a just legal justice system in place, people often took the law into their own hands. English historians were quick to document and lament atrocities committed by Scottish robbers and brigands against the English soldiers, but the same powers of observation were not granted to English crimes against the common people.

The exact timeline of Wallace's evolution from solitary outlaw to militia leader is unknown, but the consensus is that his rise in prominence occurred between 1293 and 1296. During this time, he improved his swordsmanship and athletic prowess. More crucially, he turned into a powerful military strategist that could command a relatively large force of men and lead them toward a victory against the most successful army in all of Europe at the time. Despite his lack of wealth, noble standing, formal military experience, or land ownership, Wallace's impressive physique, unwavering willpower, and charisma were enough to propel his rise from fugitive to war hero.

Blind Harry details several of Wallace's exploits from his time as an outlaw. In one instance, Wallace decided to take up an English soldier/weightlifter's challenge to let anyone strike him across the back with a rough pole in Ayr. While in disguise, Wallace accepted his challenge and then broke his back with a single blow. He then quickly killed five other English soldiers while making his escape to Leglen Wood.

In another tale, the outcome veers far closer to tragedy. Wallace was in Aur once again and decided to intervene when one of Lord Percy's men demanded a sheriff's servant to hand over a fish he had purchased for his master. Wallace killed him but was then overpowered by the sheer number of English soldiers who rushed to avenge their comrade. He was bound hand and foot and starved in a dungeon. By the time his trial came, he had contracted a fever and was in a deep coma. The English assumed he was dead and tossed his body over a wall, leaving him to rot in a heap of dung.

Thankfully, his first nurse at Ellerslie arrived and asked for the permission to give his body a proper burial. The soldiers agreed, leaving her to discover that he was still alive. She arranged for a fake wake to keep up the impression that he was dead, and secretly nursed him back to health. The news of Wallace's death became a matter of widespread significance when Thomas the Rhymer – a known prophet and soothsayer – prophesied that Wallace would play a pivotal role in restoring Scottish pride upon discovering that he was still alive:

"For sooth, ere he decease,

Shall many thousands in the field make end.

From Scotland he shall forth the Southron send,

And Scotland thrice he shall bring to peace.

So good of hand again shall ne'er be kenned[253]."

This was an age before science – an age of superstition and destiny. Thomas the Rhymer (Sir Thomas Rymour of Ercildoune) was in his seventies by this time and had accurately predicted the death of Alexander III, who had ill-fatedly decided to take a nighttime horse ride during a storm despite the prophecy of doom that hung over his head.[254] Having fought his way back to life from the dead, the prophecy would have surely empowered him with a sense of destiny and purpose. When Wallace made his recovery, he made his way to Glasgow by road with only a rusty blade for protection. Silver, horses, and armor were soon acquired by killing two English soldiers he met on the way.

He was reunited with his Uncle Richard at Riccarton. The lone outlaw was no more. As the prophesied savior of Scotland, he was joined by Sir Richard's three sons, Richard, Adam, and Simon, along with Robert Boyd of Kilmarnock and several other trusted companions. This band of brothers, nephews, uncles, cousins, and distant relatives formed a literal and figurative brotherhood that was wholly united against their formidable English foes. Wallace had become a Christ-like figure after narrowly escaping death; his fame inspired devotion, loyalty, and faith in the possibility of a victory. What the Scots lacked in technological sophistication and weaponry, they made up in zeal, inventiveness, and their acute knowledge of their home terrain.

Chapter 5 – Uprising

According to Blind Harry,[255] Wallace seized the opportunity to avenge his father's death in 1297. Wallace learned that Fenwick, the knight who had killed his father, had returned to Scotland and was preoccupied with a mission in the southwest. He had been tasked with transporting large amounts of gold and silver (which had been confiscated from the Scottish churches) to Ayr. Wallace planned an ambush at Loudoun Hill.

When he emerged from the wood, he was no longer dressed in a disguise. He wore a secure armor, a small steel helmet, gloves made of plate cloth armor, a habergeon (a chainmail neck-covering that protected the breast), and a steel collar. Since his helmet was not closed, he had to protect his face with his armored hands.

Fenwick was accompanied by one hundred and eighty men, while Wallace was now the leader of fifty men.[256] He surprised the English horsemen by blocking the narrow pass with boulders and rocks. His men forced them to fight on foot by stabbing the horses in their unarmored belly. Wallace and his lieutenants quickly dispatched of the English leaders (including Fenwick), which then demoralized the surviving soldiers. Eighty of them successfully escaped, leaving a hundred of their comrades lying dead on the ground. Many had been trampled by the horses, which panicked after their rider was eliminated. Wallace lost three men and killed all his opponents. The English servants were marched to Clyde's Forest and hung, but he made sure that his men spared all women and children. His men then took possession of two hundred horses, the provisions and wine they carried, the Knights' armor, weapons, and money.

News of the victory spread across the countryside, where it was interpreted as a sign that the prophecy was being fulfilled. Fifty Scotsmen had successfully taken down nearly two hundred horsemen despite their heavy armor. The English soldiers no longer seemed as invincible as they had once been. Other patriotic-minded young men, fugitives, and men who resented English rule began to seek out the gigantic outlaw that served as a beacon of hope against English oppression.

Meanwhile, Lord Percy was being advised to establish a truce with the growing threat. It was not uncommon for Scottish magnates to switch allegiances after being promised generous wealth and large estates. Sir Ranald Craufurd was pressured to serve as an intermediary, since Wallace was his nephew. Wallace accepted the terms of the truce, which was to last for ten months. His men then went their separate ways.

He proved to be unsuited to a quiet and peaceful life. One day, he headed into town with fifteen of his allies in disguise. There, he spotted a passage-at-arms and a famed English champion who had defeated all of his opponents thus far. When Wallace secured a quick and effortless victory, the English soldiers realized that this unusually large man was the notorious outlaw. After a violent confrontation, Wallace and his allies escaped, leaving twenty-nine dead English soldiers in the market town. Lord Percy then insisted that Wallace stay out of the town, fair, or market to avoid confrontations with his soldiers.

When Sir Ranald was summoned to attend a council at Glasgow in September 1296, Wallace got into another confrontation with the English soldiers. While riding ahead of his uncle's entourage, he encountered a few of Percy's men. They demanded that Wallace hand over Sir Ranald's pack-horse to them, leaving him livid. Wallace was further disgruntled when his uncle agreed to let the matter go. That night, he confronted the three horsemen and two-foot soldiers that had demanded the horse and killed them all with the help of two comrades. They returned with the horse, Percy's horses, harness, equipment, weapons, and money. The trio then headed to the safety of the mountains surrounding Loch Lomond.

At the council, Wallace was declared a formal outlaw and an enemy of King Edward. Sir Ranald and his troop were arrested and made to answer for the murder and robbery of Percy's men. The charges were dropped when he produced a solid alibi and insisted that he had no knowledge of Wallace's plans. He was forced to swear that he would not communicate with his nephew from that point onward.

Meanwhile, Wallace began recruiting more men until he had sixty of them under his command. With the help of his hardened fellow outlaws, he began to act as a Scottish Robin Hood. The English were killed and robbed. Their possessions were generously distributed to the Scots. Wallace headed toward the north, where he successfully captured the tower at Gargunnock. After four days, he and his men burned the castle and continued on their way to Strathearn. They killed every Englishman they met along the way.

His band of men took on Sir James Butler of Kinclaven and his men. Their numbers were evenly matched, but the English had the advantage of their horses and better armor. The Scots repeated their strategy at Loudoun Hill. By slashing at the horses' legs and bellies, they unseated the English riders and attacked them with their swords. Wallace himself slashed through Sir James' armor, cutting into his bone and brain. With their commander dead, many of the survivors panicked and fled. Wallace and his men followed them into the castle, where everyone – except the women, children, and two priests – was killed. After robbing the castle of its wealth, the survivors were freed and the castle was burned to the ground.

Lady Butler and the other survivors headed to Perth to raise the alarm. Wallace soon had a more formidable opponent: Sir Gerard Heron and his thousand-man cavalry. Wallace braced himself for the assault, ready to make a stand. The Scots had precise aim, but the English archers had a seemingly endless supply of arrows. During the battle, Wallace himself suffered an arrow shot under the neck which left him with a permanent scar. With only fifty men left standing against the English forces (whose numbers had surged with the arriving reinforcements), Wallace urged his men to fight valiantly despite being outnumbered ten to one: "Here is no choice but either do or die. We have the right with us." In the end, they were forced to retreat into the deepest and thickest parts of the woods. After a few more scuffles, they managed to escape.

After a few more close calls with the English forces, Wallace was left with only a tiny cohort. The stories about their efforts nevertheless traveled across the country, inspiring the same dedication to resistance in the minds and hearts of their countrymen. Aggrieved by the deaths of many of his comrades, Wallace kept a low profile. Blind Harry nevertheless reports that he still killed any Englishmen he encountered (in areas where there were fewer English patrolmen) during this interim period.

Chapter 6 – Love in a Time of War

In Mel Gibson's 1995 Hollywood blockbuster film *Braveheart*,[257] Wallace's transformation into a legendary hero is catalyzed by the death of his wife. Her name in the movie is Murron MacClannough, and she is portrayed by English actress Catherine McCormack. The idea of Wallace being inspired to lead his countrymen to achieve a decisive victory against the English by the attempted rape and murder of his wife is certainly highly symbolic. Her body thus becomes a vivid and visceral metaphor for the nation of Scotland itself.

The historical reality is probably far less poetic and simple. Wallace had certainly already been dedicated to opposing the English forces long before he fell in love. The original Blind Harry poem makes no mention of a wife, although it does refer to a woman named Innes. Innes is credited for helping him escape from the English troops; Blind Harry does not mention that she was his wife or lover.

In a 1570 revised edition of Blind Harry's poem, the eighteen-year-old Marion Braidfute makes her first appearance as William Wallace's wife. The plot is simple and symbolic: the Sheriff of Lanark murders Marion, encouraging Wallace to lead a successful rebellion against the English. Some historians have argued that Marion is a fictional character who was invented to support a noble family's claim to be Wallace's descendants. The revised edition conveniently mentions that Marion gave birth to a daughter before being murdered by the sheriff. Her name – which seems to draw a parallel to Robin Hood's love interest Maid Marian (or Marion) – also seems to be too symbolically convenient.

Myth or fact, Marion endures because her existence makes Wallace's narrative more compelling. According to Blind Harry, Marion herself bore a deep resentment against the English for her older brother's death. Wallace supposedly fell in love at first sight when he saw her at the Church of Saint Kentigern, near Lanark.

Despite deeming marriage in the time of war to be imprudent, Wallace began seeing Marion in secret whenever he came to town. To make matters even more imprudent, Sir William Heselrig, the English sheriff of Lanark, was interested in having Marion marry his son.

Blind Harry reports that Wallace planned to marry Marion once he had freed Scotland from English rule. In another part of the poem, however, he contradicts this pact and reveals that they did get married and produced a daughter who then married a squire named Shaw, thus preserving Wallace's lineage. Several historians – including Dr Charles Rogers – have dismissed all claims that

Wallace married or had any children, illegitimate or otherwise.[258]

In any case, Blind Harry reports that Sir William Heselrig, Sheriff of Clydesdale, accosted Wallace one Sunday morning as he left Saint Kentigern's Church. After a series of insults, Wallace and his men began fighting with Heselrig's men. Wallace had purportedly married Marion by this time, and he took refuge in her house after the Scots were forced to retreat. Heselrig and his men eventually marched up to Marion's door, demanding Wallace's surrender. Marion killed time by arguing with him, allowing Wallace to escape out the back door. When they realized what was going on, they smashed through the door and killed her then and there.

Wallace's own mother is believed to have died around this time period, creating a strong emotional incentive for him to strike a deadly blow at the English. Whatever his actual motivations and intentions, Wallace did successfully murder Sir William Heselrig in May 1297. That very night, Wallace and his men returned to town. Wallace made a straight line for the sheriff's home and found his target in the bedroom. With a single downward stroke, he cut through Heselrig's skull, right down to the collarbone. The fact that he cut the sheriff to pieces does suggest that there was a personal vendetta that had to be settled, but perhaps he was only making an example out of him to strike fear in the English forces. After killing

Heselrig's son, he burned the house and its remaining inhabitants. Wallace and his men then took the opportunity to kill many Englishmen that night – approximately 240 were murdered.

Unlike Blind Harry's reports of Wallace's exploits, the carnage at Lanark is supported by Wallace's trial documents. Wallace was specifically charged with murdering the Sheriff of Clydesdale, presumably as a symbolic action that instigated the various resistance efforts that coalesced into the first Scottish War of Independence. There had been many uprisings and revolts before this, of course, but none of them matched the scale and severity of Heselrig's murder and the Lanark massacre.

Chapter 7 – The Battle of Stirling Bridge

Wallace quickly fled to the familiar territory of Ayrshire after the Lanark massacre. Scottish men from the southwest rallied to his side, reuniting Wallace with old comrades and many fresh faces. The revolutionary spirit had been kindled, and Wallace now had the benefit of all the weapons and armor he had taken from the defeated English soldiers. At this point, he was in charge of three thousand men with decent weaponry, as well as many men without the benefit of horses and military equipment.

Gilbert de Grimsby (who was known to the Scots as Jop) had also joined Wallace's ranks. As a well-regarded soldier who had served in the English army and been recognized by no less than King Edward himself, his defection was a severe blow to the English forces. Besides his own skills and military prowess, he arrived with critical intelligence about the English army and its inner workings. Wallace happily made him his standard-bearer.

The flames of revolt were also stirred by the Robert Wishart (the Bishop of Glasgow) and James the Steward. Both men had been elected Guardians of Scotland in 1286. Wishart was opposed to Edward's attempts to anglicize the Scottish Church. This involved the replacement of Scottish clergy members with English priests. Unlike the Scottish magnates, the clergymen had no land and wealth interests to protect. Wallace certainly benefited from Wishart's network of like-minded clergymen who could use the cover of the church for covert anti-English activities and communication. With Wishart's backing, Wallace's revolt was "justified" as a legitimate war in the name of King John.

Wallace did not have to wait long for action. After he was released from confinement in late 1296, Sir Willian Douglas (previously governor of Berwick Castle) swiftly allied himself with the rebels. He attacked and captured the Sanquhar castle, and then had to defend it against the Captain of Durisdeer. Wallace rushed to the scene to aid him, killing five hundred English soldiers as a result. Edward responded by stripping Douglas of his property and lands in Northumberland and Essex. This did not stop other prominent Scottish figures – like Robert Bruce, the future King of Scotland – from defecting to the rebels.

Wallace also discovered that he had a counterpart in the northern part of the country. Andrew de Moray had decided to stage a rash revolt after his father and uncle (Sir Andrew de Moray and Sir William) were taken prisoner after the Battle of Dunbar. By April 1297, the entire area of Moray was united in opposing the English. Given that the Moray family had the same name as the region they lived in, it is no surprise that they were a powerful family with massive estates and influence. Moray and his men began attacking the English garrisons in the northeast and were eventually emboldened to attack Urquhart Castle.

Edward was away while all this was happening, and the Englishman that was nominally in charge of Scotland while he was away was Hugh Cressingham (who was based in Berwick). Luckily for the Scots, Cressingham did not carry out Edward's orders properly. There were still no stone walls at Berwick; some suspected that Cressingham was pocketing the funds for the project.

That June, Wallace raided Perth with the help of Sir Willian Douglas. Despite being at the center of the English regime in Scotland, the English defenders of Perth were forced to retreat as the Scottish army advanced. Large amounts of chattels and goods were left behind for Wallace to claim. By the end of the month, English troops in the southern part of the country had all retreated into their castles. The Scottish armed rebels roamed the countryside, confining the English to the towns and burghs. They were constantly under siege from the Scot rebels; the tables had been turned. Four critical figures were deemed to be responsible for Scotland's increasingly anarchic state: the Bishop of Glasgow, James the Steward, Andrew de Moray, and William Wallace.

Edward retaliated by ordering that all rebels be arrested and imprisoned. He rallied an army of three thousand horsemen and forty thousand footmen in the north of England and sent them across the Scottish border. Instead of fighting, the Scottish army surrendered on 7 July. The Scottish magnates were unable to establish an effective chain of command and agree on the army's leadership structure.

The magnates may have spontaneously collapsed, but Wallace's rebel army was there to stay. They attacked Lord Percy's forces with guerilla tactics, killing over five hundred English soldiers.[259] The Scottish nobles had failed to defend their country's honor, leaving Wallace and Moray to capture to lead the revolution. Wallace confronted Lord Percy's forces at Glasgow and managed to secure a victory by the middle of the day. By the end of the month, Cressingham was writing to Edward for additional funds to cope with the widespread defiance in the country. Raising the money by taxing the Scottish people was certainly not an option by now:

> Sire, let it not displease you, by far the greater part of your counties of the realm of Scotland are still unprovided with keepers, as well by death, siege, or imprisonment; and some have given up their bailiwicks, and others neither will nor dare return; and in some counties the Scots have established and placed bailiffs and ministers, so that no county is in proper order, except Berwick and Roxburgh, and this only lately.[260]

When August 1297 drew to a close, the northern part of Scotland had largely been reclaimed by Wallace and his army of rebels. Perth and Aberdeen had been easily conquered. The only exceptions were the well-defended strongholds of Dundee and Stirling. Edward ordered John de Warenne – the Earl of Surrey and Governor in Scotland for Edward – to provide additional reinforcements at Stirling and to raise the siege of Dundee.[261] As Wallace attempted to subdue the English forces at Dundee, he learned that Warenne and Cressingham were leading a large army northward toward

Stirling.[262]

Stirling is located in a central position in Scotland, making it strategically crucial. Stirling Castle was then one of the most formidable castles in the entire British Isles, perched on top of a large crag that oversaw the vast surrounding plains. The River Forth meandered through this plain, making its way toward the Scots Sea. Stirling was the gateway to the Highlands, and the English intended to recapture it to reestablish their control over the north. Led by Warenne, the English cavalry and infantry advanced toward Stirling Castle. Confident of the English army's superior numbers, weaponry, and logistics, he predicted that Wallace and Andrew de Moray's rebellion would end by defeat in battle or negotiation. His Scottish opponents were based on the Abbey Craig, which is home to the National Wallace Monument today.

The English forces eventually arrived at a narrow, wooden bridge that crossed the River Forth. The Stirling Bridge that exists today is in a different location from this original bridge. The old bridge was supported by 8 piers and was actually diagonal. The bridge was only wide enough to allow two horsemen to pass through abreast. Warenne's entire cavalry (1,000 men) and infantry (15,000 men) would have taken a few hours to get to the other side. They would then be forced to enter a narrow bend in the river, leaving them vulnerable to attacks from the side.

Given the disadvantageous terrain, Warrene did not order his troops to cross the bridge immediately. For a few days, both forces remained on opposite banks of the river. Warrene expected Wallace and Moray to surrender without a fight. He was surprised when they refused to admit defeat despite the recent English victories and their obvious military advantages. The two Dominican friars he sent across to bridge to negotiate surrender from Wallace returned with a call for confrontation: "Tell your commander that we are not here to make peace but to do battle, defend ourselves and liberate our kingdom. Let them come on, and we shall prove this in their very beards."[263]

This was certainly a brave decision. An army made up of common men had never stood up against the might of the English army before this. The forces that were led by Scottish nobility had all been defeated thus far. Wallace and Mornay were both young and experienced. The odds were against them, but they were willing to risk everything. All of them possessed a determination to bring English tyranny in their country to an end. They had endured the English soldier's brutality, arrogance, rudeness, and imperiousness over the past seven years; it was time to attempt to bring that era to an abrupt end.

Finally convinced that Wallace and Mornay would not surrender, Warenne ordered his troops to cross the bridge on the morning of the 11th of September. Warenne had considered sending his horsemen upstream to the Ford of Drip, so that they could provide protection to his footmen as they crossed the bridge. This idea was suggested by Sir Richard Lundie, a Scottish noble who had switched allegiances at the battle of Irvine:

> My lords, if we go on to the bridge we are dead men; for we cannot cross it except two by two, and the enemy are on our flank, and can come down on us as they will, all in one front. But there is a ford not far from here, where we can cross sixty at a time. Let me now therefore have five hundred knights and a small body of infantry, and we will get round the enemy on the rear and crush them; and meanwhile you, my Lord Earl, and the others who are with you, will cross the bridge in perfect safety. [264]

This plan was foiled by Cressingham, who lamented the fact that a large amount of money had already been spent to subdue the revolution. The English army was to cross immediately and acquire a swift victory. When more than half of the English army had crossed over to the other side, Wallace and Moray set the trap they had planned into action. Armed with long spears, the Scottish rebels charged down the causeway at the sound of Wallace's horn. The right flank of the charge made their way across the river bank to arrive at the bridge's north end, thus preventing the English army from retreating to safety. The English army was now trapped, but one group of English knights managed to fight their way back across the bridge. The archers would have been able to assist the English forces by firing from the other side of the river, but they had unfortunately already crossed the bridge by this point. Warenne had wisely waited to cross the bridge, and had it destroyed before retreating to Berwick.

The rest of the English army who had crossed over was then forced to defend themselves against the Scottish onslaught. Some were able to swim to safety, while others were weighted down by the heavy armor and drowned, and the large majority were killed in the massacre. Hugh de Cressingham, who had crossed first, was killed alongside the rest. From their higher vantage point on the slope, the Scottish rebels aimed their spears and other missiles onto the advancing English knights. The knights that survived were soon disoriented when they reached the marshy ground on the other side, a location which severely compromised their horses.

It was a momentous victory. Five thousand English soldiers have been killed, while the rest retreated. The well-armed and mounted English knight had been proven to be fallible at the battlefield after all and at the hands of a ragtag group of spearmen that consisted mostly of commoners. Scotland had not achieved victory against a significant English army since the times of the Dark Ages. The Battle of Stirling Bridge thus proved to be a potent catalyst for the ongoing resistance against Edward's imposition. Wallace's victory was not without casualties, however. Andrew Mornay was fatally wounded during the battle. He survived for two months before being buried at the Fortrose Cathedral.[265]

Chapter 8 – Invading England

The Battle of Stirling Bridge may have been a momentous event, but it was not enough to single-handedly force Edward to retire his designs on Scotland. Wallace's unexpected victory also created further divisions between his guerilla forces and the Scottish nobility. It was no secret that the Scottish magnates had been motivated more by their own interests rather than an inspiring sense of patriotism, and Wallace's newfound influence threatened to further weaken their positions in the eyes of the Scottish commoners.

There was nevertheless a brief window when Wallace commanded the support of Scots across all class lines. He wasted no time in attacking the remaining pockets of English resistance after his victory of Stirling. The English forces at Dundee had already learned of their counterparts' crushing defeat at Stirling and surrendered soon after Wallace and his men arrived. He then set his sights on reclaiming the rest of Scotland's rigorously fortified castles: Cupar Castle, Edinburg Castle, Dunbar Castle, Berwick Castle, and Roxburgh Castle. Wallace's forces were unable to force the defenders of the latter four castles to surrender, but they were able to force the English army out of their respective towns.

By October, Wallace had been successful in driving a large majority of the English army out of Scotland. A few castles and strongholds remained under English control, but they now exerted negligible power over the Scottish populace. This astounding achievement – which Wallace pulled off without much help from the Scottish nobility – established his reputation as a powerful general and a rising political force. In truth, Wallace's victory was shared with Andrew de Moray. Both young men were the sons of knights, but the latter was in possession of substantial lands, a status indicator that mattered significantly during the thirteenth century. With Andrew on his deathbed, however, Wallace was the sole claimant of the spoils.

As the de facto leader of Scotland, Wallace quickly communicated with Scotland's trading partners to let them know that "the kingdom of Scotland is recovered by war from the power of the English" and was ready to resume business. Wallace might have won over the common people at this point, but he still faced the difficult task of establishing an alliance with the great Scottish magnates. Some were converts to his cause, others were ambivalent, and a few were determined to support Edward. Wallace mobilized his forces to attack Earl Patrick, a staunch Edward supporter who had refused to swear his loyalty to Scotland and insulted Wallace when summoned to do so.

Once Earl Patrick had been defeated, Wallace and his forces were free to turn the tables on Berwick, which had become an English settlement after its harrowing defeat the previous year. Wallace repaid the bloody favor by allowing his army to turn the town into a scene of carnage once again. After Berwick, the Scottish forces advanced into Northumberland and Cumbria. Many Northumbrians had fled to Newcastle, which offered the protection of its fortified walls, after witnessing the once-proud and indestructible English army fleeing southward in an alarmingly disorganized manner. Since they had taken their cattle and their valuables with them, the Scots were greeted with empty farmhouses and cottages. These were quickly burned to the ground by the angry Scots.

At Cumbria, Wallace's men had to be more strategic. Instead of indiscriminate destruction, they claimed all the food they could find. Meanwhile, the Northumbrians returned to their villages and farms, as they believed that the Scottish forces had moved on. When Wallace learned of their return, he ordered his men to greet the English villagers with a nasty surprise. All the Englishmen that lived in Northumbria paid dearly for the atrocities their countrymen had inflicted on Berwick, even though they had nothing to do with the massacre.

Wallace had no intentions of ordering his men to attack the castles that were occupied by the English forces, but Carlisle was an exception. Its strategic position as the western entry point to

Scotland made it crucial in tipping the balance of military power between Wallace's army and the English army. He sent a large force to surround it, but they made no major attempt to attack its inhabitants. The rest of Wallace's vagrant army headed to Newcastle. There, they burned the small town of Ritton to the ground after its villagers made the painful mistake of taunting the Scots from across the river, not assuming that the Scots would simply swim across it.

By now, Wallace's attempt to avenge his fallen countrymen by attacking the north of England had thoroughly demoralized the northern English people. Over seven hundred English villages were burned down without mercy or remorse; Wallace's forces killed thousands of defenseless people. Those that remained had no courage or conviction to resist or defy the Scottish invaders. The Scottish army thus had free reign to strip the villages of towns of most of their food and valuable possessions.

The Scots' presence in northern England was nevertheless short-lived. Not long before Christmas that year, the English led a counterattack against the Scots. Under Sir Robert de Clifford's instructions, several thousand English foot soldiers killed over three hundred Scotsmen at Annandale. By the time they took a break for Christmas, ten villages and towns had been razed. They resumed their attacks the next year, claiming the town of Annan and destroying the Gisburn church. Civilians on both sides of the Scottish border suffered disproportionately during this time.

Chapter 9 – The Guardian of Scotland

The historical record on who actually knighted Wallace is unclear, but he was knighted Guardian of Scotland sometime around the Christmas period of 1297. Wallace was probably knighted by a member of the Scottish nobility or a powerful magnate; this may have been James the Steward or Malcolm, Earl of Lennox. In any case, Wallace now had the power to act on behalf of the entire Scottish realm and with the consent and support of the magnates. Some of the magnates undoubtedly bore some opposition to the idea of a young man of dubious standing becoming the sole ruler of Scotland, but he had won the confidence of the people and had a victorious army behind him.

At the dawn of 1298, Wallace was at the peak of his military and political career. He had an unexpected victory against the most powerful army in Europe under his belt and had returned from his northern invasion of England with large bounties of cattle, grain, and other precious food commodities. A giant in body, spirit, and reputation, he had an enviable image as a selfless patriot who had dedicated his entire life to a vision of an independent and proud Scotland. Meanwhile, the Scottish nobility – the knights, earls, and barons – had been severely discredited by their notoriously shaky allegiances.

Wallace was thus at the helm of a disorganized and divided nation, wrought by feudal hierarchies and endless infighting. As a political leader, he demonstrated the same capacity for decisive and immediate action that he showcased on the battlefield. The magnates that did not gratefully heed his commands were ruthlessly cowed into submission. At the end of the day, however, none of the Scottish earls were willing to pledge their undivided support. Blinded by envy and wounded by the idea of being outranked by a commoner, they could not put aside their self-interests to support the interests of the public.

Their temporary allegiance to Wallace was nevertheless unwavering enough to prevent them from attending a parliament session called by Edward on 14 January 1298. Their absence – which effectively marked them as public enemies of England – indicated the extent to which Edward's grip over Scotland had waned. The loyalties of England's own magnates to Edward were also under major strain. The English earls did attend that parliament session, but they were indignant at the cost that Edward's foreign invasions had inflicted upon them. Edward himself was absent, leaving behind a power vacuum that nearly led to a revolt.

Edward began raising money to pay for an imposing attack against Wallace. Welsh troops were mobilized for a decisive retaliation. By 22 January, the English magnates estimated that they had an army of fourteen thousand horsemen and a hundred thousand foot soldiers assembled, the largest army to be amassed against the Scots thus far. Anxious to redeem himself after the disastrous Battle of Stirling Bridge, Earl Warenne led the second charge into Scotland. The sheer size of the English army secured a quick victory at Roxburgh. Warenne then advanced to Kelso, where the presence of Wallace's cavalry halted their progress into the hills. They then headed to Berwick, where they were graced with another quick surrender. At Berwick, Edward communicated to Warenne that he was returning to England to take supreme command over the Scottish invasion. Warenne was to stay put until he returned.

The winter of 1297-98 was a decisive period for both sides. Wallace organized Scotland into military districts and began conscripting all able-bodied Scottish males that were older than sixteen. He established a proper chain of command that borrowed from classical Rome and Greece, doing away with the former feudal arrangements that accorded greater military prestige to the landowning classes. Instead of appointing lower-ranked members of the nobility to the clergy, military, administrators, and law enforcement, Wallace began to recruit common men like himself on the basis of their merit. He erected gallows in every town, village, and burgh – a warning of what would befall those who failed to heed his conscription regulations.

The clergy was not spared from Wallace's zeal for reform. He appointed William de Lamberton to become the head of St. Andrews, rewarding him for his early support. With his nominee in a place of power, Wallace eliminated all the English priests that Edward had installed. These English priests and nuns were forcibly removed from their positions, and some of them were killed in the process.

Most of Wallace's efforts were ultimately focused on the upcoming confrontation with Edward. Wallace had devised and perfected a new military formation to battle the English by this point: the schiltrom. His foot soldiers would utilize their impressive twelve-foot spears to form an intimidating hedgehog-like formation, with spears posed in all directions. Protected by their shields, the Scottish infantry would be better placed to confront the feared English cavalry at close quarters.

As the English army drew closer, Wallace ordered that the towns in the Lothians and Berwickshire be destroyed. All the Scottish people in these areas were evacuated to the north, leaving behind a barren countryside. King Edward returned to England as promised and began laying down meticulous plans after testing the strength of the Scottish defenses and the will of the people to resist his massive army. There were several smaller raids and conflicts before the main invasion on 25 June. To prepare for a final and utter victory over Wallace's forces, Edward arranged for provisions to be transported from Ireland to a depot at Carlisle. Supplies were amassed at ports in eastern England, ready to be shipped into Berwick and Edinburgh once they had been reclaimed.

When Edward arrived at Roxburgh on 24 June, the English army was composed of three thousand heavy cavalrymen, four thousand light horsemen, and eighty thousand foot soldiers. A majority of the footmen were hired troops from Ireland and Wales, rather than conscripted Englishmen. Edward rode ahead of this sizable army, witnessing firsthand the preemptive devastation that awaited the English at the burned ruins of the villages and farms throughout the Lothians. After putting up a fight, the castle of Dirletons (located near the coast of East Lothian) and Tantallon were conquered. The English army then marched into the heart of Scotland, ready to attack in any direction upon knowledge of where Wallace's army was located.

Chapter 10 – Defeat at Falkirk

A large army comes with massive logistical problems. As the head of approximately 87,500 men, Edward had the difficult task of ensuring that there were sufficient food supply channels to feed all of them. As they marched further into Scotland, it was severely demoralizing to witness the extent of Wallace's scorched earth strategy. The only food source that the English troops had access to came from the supply ships, which were often compromised by itinerant weather and Scottish pirates. When Edward attempted to placate the troops by distributing two hundred casks of wine (a few supply ships had arrived with ample alcohol and little food), this lead to drunken infighting between the Welsh and Englishmen. Hunger had led the morale of the English army to reach a dangerously low point.

For now, Wallace's strategy of buying his time was working. The English army was fatigued after making many long marches throughout the Scottish countryside, without being able to engage the Scottish army in any meaningful confrontation. Edward eventually ordered his men to withdraw to Edinburgh and wait for their food supplies to be restocked. On 21 July, a scout reported that Wallace's army had been sighted nearby – eighteen miles away in the Forest of Selkirk. Wallace was evidently waiting for the English to retreat before launching his offensive.

Edward made plans for an immediate confrontation. By 9 a.m. that day, the English troops were marching toward Falkirk.[266] They arrived at Linlithgow by nightfall. The next day, they spotted the presence of a Scottish cavalry patrol. The morning sun had reflected off their spears, emitting a telltale flash. The Scots were nowhere to be found by the time the English arrived at the location, but Edward knew that the Scottish army was close by.

In retrospect, it was ill-advised for Wallace to abandon his guerrilla tactics in favor of a direct confrontation at this point. This may not have been Wallace's intention; it could very well be that the English surprised him with their willingness to march through the night. Falkirk was surrounded by more open country, making a retreat much more treacherous than in hillside terrain. Whatever the reason, Wallace ordered his troops to assemble in battle formation in a strategic location.

Historians have hazarded that the battle took place north of the actual town, on particularly marshy terrain that thwarted the English horsemen. Wallace expected a familiar set-up: his spear-armed infantry against the English's heavily armed horsemen. At Stirling, his men had been on the offensive. Here, they would be on the defensive. The site of the battle was not as advantageous as that fateful narrow bridge, but the marshes and woods did offer protection if retreat was necessary.

What Wallace could not have expected, however, was the deadliness of the Welshmen and Lancastrians' longbow. This was a recent invention that was as revolutionary to medieval warfare as poison gas had been to early twentieth century warfare. Without the deadly range and aim of the English archers, Edward's troops would likely have been thwarted by the forest of spears that the Scotsmen had organized.

As the English army drew near, Wallace compelled his men to courageous action: "I have brought you to the ring; dance the best you can!"[267] Edward initially ordered that the Welshmen be sent first into battle with the Scots, but they refused to be used as guinea pigs. In the end, the English cavalry was sent to do battle with Wallace's men, only to be surprised by the swampy grounds which had been camouflaged by the green meadow. They were forced to free themselves from the bog and find their way around it.

The second line of cavalry advanced more warily. They headed in a diagonal direction toward the eastern side of the swamp. Once they crossed the stream, they waited for the third line – led by Edward himself – to advance. Wallace's schiltroms were prepared for all four lines of English cavalry. His footmen were disciplined enough to hold tight to their spears and armor as the armed English knights advanced, forcing them to wheel about without striking the Scots.

Unable to confront the Scottish infantry, the English cavalry turned their attention toward the Scottish archers. While over a hundred English horses were claimed by the Scots spears, the English knights made quick work of the Scottish archers. Edward then ordered the core of his infantry to attack. Their ranks contained a sizable number of Lancastrian longbowmen who were able to attack where the cavalry could not reach. They summoned forth a fatal hail of arrows, backed by the flurry of stones and rocks hurled forward by the foot soldiers. The seemingly impregnable schiltroms began to flounder as they were showered with arrows and projectiles. As they abandoned their ranks and fled, the English cavalry moved in with a deadly charge. The twelve-foot spears were practically useless in close combat.

Covered by the dense woods, Wallace and the surviving members of his army retreated to the north. Upon witnessing the infantry's crushing defeat, the Scottish cavalry had wisely decided to flee to live and fight the English another day. The retreating Scottish foot soldiers were given no quarters by the English knights. Those who escaped the deadly lances were also at risk at drowning when they attempted to cross the River Carron. By the end of the chase, nearly ten thousand Scottish foot soldiers have been killed. Nearly every family in southern Scotland would have suffered grief due to this catastrophic defeat. Wallace was left without an infantry, and without his reputation as an effective Scottish leader that stood a chance of freeing Scotland from English influence. His government – which lasted for three hundred days – was brought to an abrupt end. He lived on long after Falkirk was over (unlike in the Hollywood movie, which had him tried and executed soon after this defeat), but his ability to influence Scottish affairs had been maimed.

Chapter 11 – An Outlaw Once More

Wallace gave up his guardianship soon after the Battle of Falkirk. It is not known whether this was voluntary or otherwise. In any case, his position of leadership had been severely compromised by the crushing defeat at Falkirk, despite the fact that he could not have possibly foreseen the novel deadliness of the English longbow at the time. He marched north to Stirling, where he arranged for the town and castle to be destroyed – rather than let it fall into English hands. He repeated this strategy in Perth, forcing the English to rely solely on the food brought in by their supply ships.

In August, Edward advanced into an empty and burned Ayr, without having managed to lay his hands on Wallace. When the supply ships he expected from Ireland and west England failed to arrive, his army suffered from a fifteen-day famine. By the next month, Edward had abandoned all his plans to wipe out the Scottish resistance forces. Instead, he began garrisoning various strongpoints to help cement his reign of power in Scotland.

Edward returned to England on 8 September, disappointed by the costs he had endured to achieve the victory at Falkirk. He had lost a large number of men to illness, starvation, and disease. Only a small number of his horses had returned safely to Carlisle. His troops had been on the verge of mutiny due to the lack of food, and he had not managed to destroy the Scottish rebels after all. There were, however, some consolations. They divided the estates of the Scottish barons who had failed to demonstrate their loyalties, and then restored the English clergy who had been removed from their positions in Scotland.

The worse blow was the discovery that some of Scottish magnates (e.g. Sir Simon Fraser) that had previously been very loyal to Edward were now changing sides. The English may have defeated Wallace's men, but they had also been forced into a humiliating retreat. The Scottish spirit of resistance was still burning strongly, its heat rising from the common people to the ranks of the Scottish nobility. Edward certainly did not resign himself to this state of affairs. He began making plans for another intervention, "to go forward in the Scottish business upon the enemies of the crown and realm of England, and to put down their disobedience and their malice which purpose nothing else but to subdue the said crown, and the estate of the said realm of England, to their power."[268]

Meanwhile, Wallace had melted into the woods once again, with his brother, Sir Malcolm, the Earl of Atholl, and a few other knights. Now that he could no longer lead the Scottish rebels in open warfare against Edward's forces, he had to revert back to the guerrilla tactics that he had mastered during his earlier years. His influence and impact were severely limited after the Battle of Falkirk, but he persevered instead of surrendering or admitting defeat. The duties of the Guardian of Scotland were shared by four figures during this time: Sir Robert de Keith, Sir David de Graham, and Sir William de Balliol, as well as the enigmatic James the Steward. With the Scottish magnates in the highest positions of power, the other earls, barons, and knights had less reason to oppose or undermine them. Wallace may have been removed from the picture, but he had triggered a rejuvenated sense of patriotism in the nation's traditional ruling classes.

Despite the ambivalent feelings that the Scottish elite held toward Wallace, there was no denying that he had proven to the entire nation that the Scottish spirit stood a chance against the most powerful army in all of Europe. Courage, determination, and strategic usage of the land were evidently potent enough to thwart and usurp Edward's obnoxious and intolerable subjugation of the country. If a relatively unknown man with no land to his name was brave enough to stand up against the English, why should the Scottish nobility be unable to match – or surpass – him? All they needed to do was to be united in arms against a common foe.

It is not known if Wallace had much or any faith in the ability of the new Guardians to resist and defy Edward. Whatever his outlook, it was evident that the highlight of his life and career had occurred in 1299; everything that followed appeared to be anticlimactic. Historian Ronald McNair-Scott dismissively characterized the last seven years of Wallace's life as obscure and impotent. Wallace was reduced to "harrying the English whenever he could with bands of fearless men or acting as messenger to the King of France or His Holiness the Pope for his friend William Lamberton, Bishop of St Andrews."[269] The full scope of Wallace's actions is not known, but there is sufficient documentation to demonstrate that Wallace benefited from having previously secured William de Lamberton's election to the bishopric of St. Andrews. Lamberton maintained his friendship with Wallace after the latter resigned from his Guardianship and proceeded to entrust him with diplomatic missions of the highest order.

As a diplomat, Wallace's ultimate goal was to secure the alliance of a powerful foreign nation that could help Scotland fend off Edward's plans to dominate it. Lamberton, Wallace, and a few other companions successfully evaded the English ships to sail to France and back. They were warmly received by King Philip, although the monarch did not explicitly promise to support Scotland with the French army or by allocating any significant financial resources to Scotland's fight for independence. Instead, Philip left them with a letter that praised "their constancy to their king and their shining valor in defense of their native land against injustice," and claimed that he was "not unmindful of the old league between their king, themselves, and him, and carefully pondering ways and means of helping them."[270]

Wallace was also singled out by the French monarch in a personal letter for his undying efforts to resist Edward's intimidating forces:

> Philip, by the grace of God, King of the French, to my loved and faithful, my agents, appointed to the Roman court, greetings and love: We command you to request the supreme Pontiff to hold

our loved William the Waleis, of Scotland, knight, recommended to his favor, in those things which with him he has to dispatch.

Given at Pierrefonds, on Monday after the feast of All Saints.[271] After leaving France, Wallace headed to Norway and Rome with the intention of securing the alliance of Eric II and the Pope. Wallace's diplomatic efforts did not go unnoticed by Edward. Bishop Lamberton had made a direct appeal to the papacy, and Scotland's quest for sovereign status had been treated with sympathy. By 1302, Edward was anxious at the prospect of a Scottish victory and the return of the exiled John Balliol as the King of Scotland.

This did not come to be. The Scottish elites' inability to put forth a united front proved to be highly detrimental to the entire nation once again. The Comyns, who were supporters of Balliol, effectively sidelined the Bruces. When faced with the unwanted likelihood of Balliol returning to rule Scotland, they defected to Edward I. Scotland's diplomatic efforts also proved to be at an end. The Pope needed Edward's assistance in his latest crusade against Islam to a greater degree than he needed the Scots. After his first wife, Eleanor, died in 1290, Edward negotiated a peace treaty with France and sealed it with his marriage to Marguerite, King Philip's

seventeen-year-old sister. When King Philip and Pope Boniface[272] engaged in an open war against each other, Lamberton could have only reacted in dismay (the Pope was eventually captured by the French and put to death). Balliol had to consign himself with the realization that his return was illusory after all by 1304. Fatigued by a crushing diplomatic defeat and seven years of war (Edward had been sending his troops to attack Scotland every year), the Scottish nobility were ready to cut a deal with Edward.

Edward was in an indulgent and relatively generous state of mind as he accepted the Scottish's leaders' submission to him. He rewarded the Scottish magnates that submitted to his rule with public offices in Scotland, eager to obtain their loyalty in reward. He had hoped that

Wallace himself would swear allegiance, but Wallace and his followers were willing to stand alone in their defiance. Angered by the capitulation he witnessed all around him, Wallace bravely maintained his stance as a patriot of the highest order:

> Scotland, desolate as you are, you believe too much in false words and are too unwary of woes to come! If you think like me, you would not readily place your neck under a foreign yoke. When I was growing up I learned from a priest who was my uncle to set this one proverb above all worldly possessions, and I have carried it in my heart,
>
> *I tell you the truth, freedom is the finest of things;*
>
> *Never live under a servile yoke, my son.*
>
> And that is why I tell you briefly that even if all Scots obey the King of England so that each one abandons his liberty, I and my companions who wish to be associated with me in this matter shall stand up for the liberty of the kingdom. And (may God be favorable to us!) we others shall obey no one but the King [of Scots] or his lieutenant.[273]

Chapter 12 – The Execution

Edward placed a bounty of three hundred marks on Wallace's head. When Bishop Lamberton (Wallace's old friend and loyal ally) and Sir Simon Fraser also submitted to Edward, Wallace had no powerful allies left. With a reward on his head and antagonism from all the Scottish nobles who had capitulated to English rule, Wallace had abysmal chances at defeating the English army in battle.

Wallace and his band of guerrillas were violently defeated in a battle with a large English force led by Sir William de Latimer at Happrew, Sir John de Segrave, and Sir Robert de Clifford (near Stobo). The defeat was made all the more bitter by the fact that it was a Scotsman who had tracked Wallace down for the promise of a financial reward from Edward. This was Wallace's final battle. He was in no position to help Stirling Castle – the last Scottish stronghold holding out against the English – defend itself from a full-forced English assault.

On the 1st of April 1304, Edward ordered that Stirling Castle be blockaded, preventing its defenders from gaining access to crucial provisions. Formidable siege-engines were shipped from Edinburgh to Berwick; the castle's formidable defenses would soon have to contend with the greatest artillery in the entire English Isles. On 22 April, Edward himself arrived at Stirling to lead the siege operations. He had thirteen of the most powerful devices engineered at the time, each capable of hurling forth a stone or rock that was up to three hundred pounds over a distance of a thousand yards. There was also a crane with a mobile platform that could hoist a cage of twenty men over the castle walls. Other specialized machines were equipped to pull down parapets and galleries, while others were designed to ram through gates and walls.

The defenders of Stirling Castle had no intentions of going down without a fight. They lowered grapnels from the walls with cranes, overturning Edward's specialized machines. Molten lead and boiling oil rained down on the English army. Edward himself was shot by a Scottish archer but was saved by his armor. The English army was also plagued by the same lack of food as the Scottish defenders; their horses had to subsist on grass alone. On 20 July 1304, the Scottish rebels finally succumbed to Edward's demand for an absolute and unconditional surrender. Sir William Oliphant was imprisoned in the Tower of London, leaving Wallace standing alone as the country's last great patriot. Edward offered fairly lenient terms to the Scottish magnates that had opposed him. They were humiliated in public, banished for a few years, or sent into exile.

While Edward tightened his grip over the country with a more intrusive military and administrative occupation, Wallace led his band of outlaws through the countryside. Their main concerns were survival. They had to secure enough supplies while eluding the English army and Scotsmen eager to turn them in for Edward's bounty. Edward may have been merciful to the magnates, but he appeared to harbor an obsessive hatred for Wallace. He had the Scottish leaders hunt Wallace down; their success in capturing him would allow them to obtain a more lenient punishment from him:

> The King will see how they bear themselves in the business and will show more favor to the man that shall have captured Wallace, by shortening his term of exile, by diminishing the amount of his ransom or of his obligation for trespass, or by otherwise lightening his liabilities. It is further ordained that the Steward, Sir John de Soulis and Sir Ingram de Umfraville shall not have any letters of safe-conduct to come into the power of the King until Sir William Wallace shall have surrendered to him.
> [274]

Despite the tantalizing incentive, none of these men decided to hunt down Wallace. Wallace was an elusive fugitive for two years, as Scotland endured the indignity of all the English constables, sergeants, sheriffs, provosts, tax-gatherers, officials, and soldiers that swarmed through the country, hell-bent on restoring law and order. The rebellious and defiant spirit that the common people had once exhibited had been tamed, leaving behind a docile and submissive populace.

Wallace stood out as a sore thumb in this landscape. The story of his downfall is especially painful to Scottish patriots since he was ultimately betrayed by a fellow Scotsman. The villain in this narrative is Sir John de Menteith,[275] a knight from one of the most eminent Norman families in Scotland. He had switched sides several times during Scotland's war of independence and had recently returned to Edward's service in September 1303. Edward personally selected him to capture Wallace because Menteith knew Wallace personally. Wallace was an intimate friend and the godfather to Menteith's two sons. This treachery was doubly painful since Menteith had once been highly regarded as a leader of the patriots.

According to Blind Harry, Menteith was reluctant to execute his mission until Edward sent him a personal letter. Menteith then assigned his nephew to join Wallace's band of guerillas so that he could be informed of their movements. When he received news that Wallace had rode out to Robroyston in hopes of meeting Robert Bruce – the man he hoped could restore Scottish independence – Menteith swiftly headed in that direction with sixty of his most loyal men. Wallace was purportedly apprehended at night from the bed he shared with his mistress. Kerly, Wallace's right-hand man, was brutally killed on the spot.

Wallace attempted to fight off Menteith's men with his bare hands (his weapons had been stolen as he slept), but he was hopelessly outnumbered. Blind Harry claims that Menteith then deceived Wallace to get him to surrender, claiming that they were surrounded by a formidable number of English knights and Barons, but that he would be under his protection at Dumbarton Castle. Wallace naively agreed to be bound hand and foot. Upon exiting his tent and seeing Kerly's corpse – and no English army in sight – Wallace realized that he had been tricked.

Menteith was handsomely rewarded with a grant of valuable land, royal favor, and gratuity. In 1306, he was granted the title and earldom of Lennox. Edward had made intricate plans for Wallace to be captured alive so that he could stage a humiliating death that would diminish the power of his reputation. Wallace would not be executed in the Scottish countryside; he would be taken to London for a show trial and the most grotesque manner of death that a medieval mind could imagine. His journey out of the country was made in great secret so as to discourage the possibility that his men or the common people of Scotland might impulsively attempt to free their beloved hero.

Wallace's reputation preceded him in England. Large crowds amassed to watch and jeer at the gigantic young man who had been such a feared enemy in Scotland. The English propaganda machine had painted him as "an ogre of unspeakable depravity who skinned his prisoners alive, burned babies and forced the nuns to dance naked for him." He was also thoroughly decried as a rapist of nuns, a torturer of priests, a mutilator of English soldiers, and arsonists of women and children. Wallace was placed in a heavily guarded house the night he arrived in London, a temporary stop before his trial at Westminster Hall the following morning. His fate may have already been decided by Edward, but the trial was necessary to make a forceful impression on the people of England and Scotland, as well as French sympathizers and the Papacy.

Wallace was swiftly found guilty of sedition, homicide, robbery, arson, sundry, and other crimes. His murder of William de Heselrig, Sheriff of Lanark, was singled out as concrete evidence of his attempt to lead a rebellion against Edward, the "rightful" lord of Scotland. He had also inflicted atrocious cruelties on the English counties of Northumberland, Cumberland, and Westmorland, where he failed to exempt children, women, priests, nuns, churches, and religious relics from violence and destruction. There was no need for witnesses to be examined, for Wallace to be defended by a lawyer, or for the judges to deliberate. Wallace was not even granted the opportunity of defending himself. He did, however, insist on making the crowded hall hear him as he argued that he could not be guilty of treason since he had never pledged his allegiance to Edward.

The punishment that Wallace suffered may seem especially heinous, but it was actually fairly standard procedure for those found guilty of treason during this period. Wallace was stripped naked and drawn by two horses from the Palace of Westminster to the Tower of London, to Aldgate, and through the city to the Elms. As he endured this intentionally long-winded route, the Londoners flung garbage and excrement at him. He was hanged, and then taken down from the gallows before his neck was broken. His genitals were sliced off. He was disemboweled; his intestines were pulled out and burned. The executioner then pulled out his internal organs – the liver, the lungs, etc. – before finally killing Wallace by ripping out his heart. The mob cheered as his head was cut off with a cleaver. The hanging, mutilation, disemboweling, and climactic decapitation was intended to inflict incomparable pain, degradation, and humiliation. His body was cut into four quarters. His head was hung up on the London Bridge, while the four quarters were sent to Newcastle-upon-Tyne, Berwick, Stirling, and St. Johnson "as a warning and a deterrent to all that pass by and behold them."

Printed in Great Britain
by Amazon